HOW TO LEAD A THRIVING SCHOOL

A Step by Step Guide for Elementary Principals Creating a Culture that Helps all Staff and Students to Thrive

Marg Dodds

BALBOA.PRESS
A DIVISION OF HAY HOUSE

Balboa Press books may be ordered through booksellers or by contacting:

Balboa Press
A Division of Hay House
1663 Liberty Drive
Bloomington, IN 47403
www.balboapress.com
844-682-1282

Because of the dynamic nature of the Internet, any web addresses or links contained in this book may have changed since publication and may no longer be valid. The views expressed in this work are solely those of the author and do not necessarily reflect the views of the publisher, and the publisher hereby disclaims any responsibility for them.

The author of this book does not dispense medical advice or prescribe the use of any technique as a form of treatment for physical, emotional, or medical problems without the advice of a physician, either directly or indirectly. The intent of the author is only to offer information of a general nature to help you in your quest for emotional and spiritual well-being. In the event you use any of the information in this book for yourself, which is your constitutional right, the author and the publisher assume no responsibility for your actions.

Any people depicted in stock imagery provided by Getty Images are models, and such images are being used for illustrative purposes only. Certain stock imagery © Getty Images.

ISBN: 978-1-9822-7992-9 (sc)
ISBN: 978-1-9822-7993-6 (e)

Print information available on the last page.

Balboa Press rev. date: 02/01/2023

Here's What Marg's Colleagues Have to Say:

"Working with Marg was a Master's class in connection. Her leadership drew from an intuitive knowing that relationships are the core of educational programs. Hers was a personal paradigm, where all students, parents, educators, care staff, support staff were seen and valued."

- Irma Di Renzo (Early Childhood Educator in a School Family Centre)

"Only listen to Marg Dodds' advice if you want to be pushed to your best self. She is a master at viewing the big picture. She digs into her tool kit for brilliant solutions and practical resources that result in CHANGE. These changes will produce happy, successful students and staff, and informed, satisfied communities."

- Charlene Frankavitz (Principal and Special Education Teacher)

"Working in an environment that is nurtured by positivity, creates opportunities for people to feel safe, valued, heard, and that they contribute to the school community as a greater whole. As humans, the need to feel valued and that we matter is intrinsic. When this is demonstrated by the leadership in the school, and a positive mindset is the starting point, safe professional environments are created to solve the difficult challenges. Positive leadership is leading by example: with your words, actions, and mindset demonstrating "we got this, we will do this together." In today's current social, political, and environmental climates the leaders who create these environments are crucial to the positive progressive change in how we think and feel about the world and those around us."

- Cass Swift (Special Education Teacher)

"I have driven school buses for over 30 years, and I have never encountered a principal as hands on or practical as Marg Dodds. Whenever I had a problem, Marg worked with me, the school, the parents, and most of all the student to come to a successful resolution."

- Phil Burnford (School Bus Driver)

"Relationships matter to Marg. She has many years of walking the talk setting up a positive school culture and climate. She can pull people together to work as a team. All aspiring principals or current principals who want to learn more about building relationships and creating a culture of caring should read this book."

- Patti Aelick (Principal)

Dedicated to my two brilliant sons,
Nicholas and Zachary.

Nick and Zac are compassionate,
caring gentlemen.

And to my husband Tom, who has supported all my adventures.
Throughout, he has been a great sport with all my shenanigans!

They make the world a better place.

Contents

About the Author

My Leadership Perspective

Kids are like sponges. They sense every interaction between the people in their lives as they try to find their way. All of us want our children, grandchildren, nieces, nephews, neighbours, and future generations to realize their full potential, equipped with the skills to navigate their life's path. Whatever life throws at them, we want them to be resilient, courageous, and resourceful as they find solutions to live fulfilling and happy lives. Ideally, we want them to be kind and compassionate too.

As Principals, we serve as role models for the children in our care and for our colleagues. We may forget this at times, but they never do. Our primary students absorb our every mood and word daily. The senior students and support staff are witness to them too. That is how we all learn what is okay and not okay, whether we're six or 45 years old.

I have loved all my jobs in education and really enjoyed the people I worked with. I was fortunate to be a teacher for grades one through eight, over 20 years, on four continents. I have also been a principal at seven different schools over the last two decades, achieving favourable results every year. Through this experience I came to realize that I had a strong, integrated education philosophy driving everything – my leadership style, interactions with kids and parents, schedules, and problem resolution – everything.

My philosophy is predicated by my own values and beliefs, along with reading everything I could get my hands on concerning leadership, conflict resolution and what strategies had the best learning outcomes for children. It requires a broad 360° view of how to help kids succeed, like finding local resources available to assist and support them.

For example, I have asked the local health unit to participate in monthly Healthy School Committee meetings. I have also organized workshops for parents, where the local family service agency made presentations on parenting strategies (such as Triple P, "Positive Parenting: Raising Resilient Children"). The goal is always to develop and maintain a thriving school environment.

This philosophy aligns with a set of educational principles that have guided my success in leading schools. Together, they led me to design and apply a set of strategies and tactics that bring these principles to life.

A number of years ago, I was invited to present a workshop at an International Confederation of Principals Conference in Australia. I prepared a presentation that explained how to implement these strategies and tactics. The presentation described my "formula" for success, which is now contained in this manual.

Introduction

My Goal as Principal

As we all know, the principal sets the tone for the school.

As a principal of 20 years, the tone I strove to set was a school in which all students and staff thrived.

My goal was to provide a school environment that helped ensure every student, upon graduation, had healthy self-esteem, self-confidence, and believed in their ability to learn and navigate their world well equipped to make good choices for themselves. Students were given opportunities to develop skills in collaboration, resiliency, perseverance, conscientiousness, compassion, curiosity, creativity, and courtesy. Through this experience students also learned to take responsibility for their own words and actions. In the seven schools where I served as principal, we were able to make remarkable progress in achieving the goal of creating a thriving school environment.

The purpose of this manual is to share how I did it and how I know you can do it too. It is divided into two sections.

The **first section** describes my leadership philosophy, and the principles, that provide the foundation to achieve this goal. In other words, they are the "what" and the "why".

The **second section** is focused on the tactics and strategies to ensure a principal is able to achieve this goal. In other words, the "how". As you will see, each of these strategies intertwine with the other. Once the strategies are in place they will weave together and build on each other. All are open, transparent communication practices.

I wish you much joy on your journey doing the work you do every day. You are setting many ripples in motion that will help make the world a better place. All the best on your fabulous adventure leading the leaders of tomorrow.

Please Note:
A series of sample templates are included at the end of this book
to further illustrate the strategies and tactics described.

The templates can also be downloaded from my website at
www.margdodds.com and modified for your school.

SECTION ONE

Philosophy

The foundation of my philosophy centres around the inherent worth of every person. For this reason, relationships and connections are incredibly important to me. I have witnessed the powerful impact that a kind or encouraging word has on all of us, whether we are a child or an adult. Sometimes we must dig deep to find the "gold" in another person. Yet, if we are persistent, the gold is always there, masked perhaps by a personality developed from trauma, loneliness, or some other hidden issue.

This deep sense that every individual matters informs my leadership. As principals, it is easy to get caught up in many competing priorities. They can distract us from our real work, which is building relationships. When we have an authentic connection with every person, we can solve conflicts and issues with relative ease. The time investment required to build such connections can seem formidable, between meetings, crisis, paperwork, and pressure. It is worth the time invested. The conflicts and issues become easier to resolve with everyone familiar with consistent expectations.

Courtesy and respect cannot be demanded. They are earned. It must be consistently demonstrated and taught to enable students to reach their full potential.

In my view everyone working and interacting with our students at school are peers. Everyone has a role to play in creating a welcoming workspace that creates the kind of culture that helps kids realize their potential. Everyone matters – from the crossing guards, bus drivers and breakfast volunteers, to the custodians and secretaries. I feel that demonstrating courtesy and respect to all these people is vital. Although I knew I was 'the boss", I never thought of myself as "better". Every person in the school can be a leader, including the kids. As principal, you have the opportunity to shine light on all the other leaders that surround you.

Academic achievement is necessary for students to have choices at the end of their time in high school – before heading into the workforce, post-secondary education, or whatever path they choose. At the elementary level we establish the groundwork for their success.

In the 21st century, we now have other non-academic predictors of success. The workplace now requires collaborative workers. More and more we need people who are persistent, creative, resilient, conscientious, kind, and compassionate. I have high expectations in all of these areas for all staff and students.

My philosophy is grounded on the basis that our education system must do its best to ensure that all kids are equipped to do what they really want to do. Students must be well informed and prepared to make choices on how they want to contribute to our communities as adults, whether they aspire to be a shopkeeper, tattoo artist, doctor, welder, or caregiver. The principal plays a key role in supporting the education system in doing its job in helping our kids to get there. Every child matters.

To bring my leadership philosophy to life, I developed principles to bring out every child's potential. These principles and accompanying strategies are described in the chapters that follow. These in turn are followed by a four-step process to implement them in your school.

Principles and Strategies

1. Self-Esteem and Self-Confidence

Self-Esteem

How a child perceives him or herself is a huge predictor of success later in life. Everything is rooted in self-esteem. Self-esteem is about how we see ourselves. It influences how we interact with everyone around us, our emotions, feelings, and thoughts. Psychologists can predict which kids are at higher risk of addiction later in life as early as kindergarten.

Children who are encouraged to take chances and feel supported even when they make mistakes will naturally grow in their self-esteem. They are far more likely to take a chance if they are not made to feel as if they have let themselves or anyone else down. Over time they will increasingly appreciate that mistakes are an opportunity to learn and a necessary process in their personal growth. They will develop a mindset that enables them to get on with things and experiences. Good teachers (and your building is full of them) help their students manage failure and overcome disappointments. Rather than giving up, students learn how to learn from their mistakes and disappointments in all areas of their lives.

Every teacher in your building can help students reach their potential with their self-esteem intact by giving them a voice in their classrooms. Give each student your undivided attention to express them-selves and let them know how important they are to you! Talk with them on the playground, in the hallway, when students are entering and exiting the classroom, gym or library, getting ready for the bus. These are GOLDEN OPPORTUNITIES to help optimize how the child will learn in the classroom, on the playground and on field trips.

Self-Confidence

Confidence is the other highest indicator of student success. (Self-esteem being the highest.) Many global studies have found this to be true, no matter what the cultural or economic background. This is something we have known in education for over 30 years.

Confidence is about belief in our abilities. It's the acknowledgement that we are all good at some things! It may be a great guitar player, soccer player, public speaker, or caregiver.

Confidence builds stronger, healthier, happier communities. All students need to feel that they are contributing members to their school community. Having this belief will carry on with them as adults - as caring citizens and part of the wider community.

Teachers help to build confidence by celebrating successes and recognizing the value of learning from mistakes. Always treat mistakes as a learning opportunity to grow. A mistake or failure does not define the child's ability. The willingness to learn from it does.

2. Physical Environment

Tour your school. The physical environment in a place of learning is EXTREMELY important. Bring a clipboard and floor plan with you. The school needs to be bright, cheerful, and welcoming!

This is one of your first tasks as a new administrator. While there may be many things that can be done at little or no cost (e.g., switching displays or notices), you will likely need to spend money to refresh the school's appearance and thereby improve the learning environment. These are necessary and worthwhile investments of effort and resources. All staff, parents and students will sense the renewed atmosphere when they walk in the building.

Note areas on the floorplan where kids may get jammed up in the hallways as they line up for dismissal, recess, going to the gym or outside the breakfast room and library. These hallway walls offer venues for teachable moments. Place motivational posters in all these places. Mindset and positive attitudes are such large predictors of success in every aspect of life. It is our responsibility to encourage them every chance we get.

There are many sources of motivational signage and posters. You can organize and order these long before your staff and students return to school. A great resource that has both positive messages and indigenous teachings is the Native Reflections website: nativereflections.ca. Another resource is Positive Promotions website: positivepromotions. com. All can be ordered on-line.

You will need a line in your school budget to enhance your school environment. If you are an administrator coming into a school part way through the year, you may want to hold off until you get to know your staff and community. You may be fortunate enough to walk into a school that already has a welcoming atmosphere. In this case, all you must do is tour the school and perhaps remove outdated information and switch around the framed posters that are already there to give it a fresh feel.

3. Safety

It is vital that kids feel safe at school.

All students and staff need to feel safe and secure to perform at their best. We need to create a safe, welcoming, and relaxing atmosphere each and every day at our schools. Each individual in our school needs to be in a circumstance that their full potential can be reached. We should try our best to make our schools warm and inviting, so our students feel safe and comfortable. This helps the brain to relax.

We are fortunate in education today that there has been so much research done on how our brains work. Neuroscientists like Dr. Jill Bolte Taylor have told us how the limbic system works. The limbic system is the part of the brain involved in our behavioural and emotional responses especially these necessary for survival. If the fear/rage response is triggered, the students brain reacts with anxiety and can only focus on the immediate situation, (fight, flight, or freeze).

We have an amygdala on each side of the brain, which are part of the brain's limbic system. The amygdala coordinates our response to what is going on in our environment, especially those that trigger an emotional response. When the brain is relaxed, the amygdala is calm, and the child is able to learn and memorize new information.

These responses are often unconscious until we learn to read our body's reactions to different stimuli or situations. Young school children are just developing this skill. As educators, we must constantly try to keep our students from feeling stressed or threatened in any way. Otherwise, their brains automatically go into self-preservation mode, and the amygdala triggers a state of anxiety. It is impossible for a child to learn in an anxious state.

It benefits all involved for all staff to give children time to calm down before being spoken to about an incident. Their brains are still in defense mode. They need time to know they are safe, and you are there to help them sort out whatever has taken place.

This is true of all people over the age of two. All students and staff in our buildings need to know they are safe, and they need to feel confident that they are being cared for appropriately.

Sensory information is coming at us all the time. In a busy classroom, your brain is processing all the other people's actions. The sensory information creates feelings in us before we can use the higher thinking of our cerebral cortex. These feelings include sadness, anger, joy, frustration, or excitement.

Well-organized and calm classrooms result in better student achievement. It is a simple fact that the children in such classrooms have experienced a limbic system that is in a calm state, which allows the cerebral cortex to focus on learning rather than distractions. Predictable routine is another huge factor in keeping the brains of our students in a calm and receptive mode. A great classroom encourages self-regulation.

Signage to be Posted in Each Classroom and Hallway

The purpose of having this signage hang in each classroom is to promote a consistent set of expectations throughout the school. They serve to reinforce the school's focus on safety. Teachers can easily reference them when dealing with minor disruptions between classmates. Soon the kids from JK up start to use this process to deal with minor conflicts between students. It is simple and quick and saves the teacher from having to mediate resolvable issues that arise daily between kids.

In each classroom, create a small display with the following: HAPPY, SAFE, HANDS OFF, IGNORE/Give space, TALK, and SEE A TEACHER. My mentor set me up with this idea during my first year as a principal and I have used them ever since.

In support of this Safety principle, a key communications tactic is for the principal to review this messaging at the "Welcome Back Assembly" and explain the importance of having the signage in each classroom. Teachers are also encouraged to follow-up, review and answer any questions about the key messages and signage. The following is an explanation for you to share with everyone.

HAPPY

If you are not feeling happy, you're not able to learn, and we want you to have your best year ever!

SAFE

When we do not feel safe, we get distracted and stressed. Our body pumps the stress hormone cortisol through our systems. This distracts us from concentrating on what we are doing in the classroom. It is REALLY important that you feel SAFE. At this time, I ask a tall Grade 8 and a Junior Kindergartener to come up to the front of the gym with me. I have them stand side by side and say to the Grade 4 to 8 students:

> "Do you remember when you were in kindergarten how scary it was to bump into a grade 8 because they were so much bigger than you?"

Usually, I get a loud "Yeah!". Then I turn to the grade 8 student and say to him or her in front of everyone:

"Would you ever do anything to hurt this little guy?"

The answer is always no. Then I ask:

"If he was crying, would you stop and ask if you could help?"

This plants the seed for the entire student body. We are all here to help each other, no matter what our age or size. Then I ask the little kindergartner:

"Do you have any reason to be afraid of this guy?"

The answer is no.

"If you see another younger person, can you please say hello to help them feel comfortable, safe and cared for in our building?"

"Kids, thank you. You can go sit down now."

By bus time that day, you will see older kids helping the little ones to get on the bus. Just plant the seed.

HANDS OFF

I simply explain to all the students that when we are trying to keep all ### students (e.g., number of students in your school) safe while playing on a playground, we must have different rules that we would not normally require for a few children playing in someone's backyard. Some rules are hard to follow, like not throwing snow, but the only way staff at the school can keep everyone safe is by having all students help us. This means not pushing, shoving, playing fighting, swearing or name calling.

Then I ask the students, if someone has trouble following these rules in the hallways, on the playground, or during gym time, what do you think we should do? They come up with great solutions! Again, your own school code of conduct and safety plans will dictate consequences. (I describe the ones I used in the Family handbook.)

IGNORE / GIVE SPACE

I explain to the students (and staff) that sometimes, people have bad days. There are (state ##) students plus (state ##) staff members. That is a lot of people together every day. I explain that if a classmate was up late because a baby was crying, or their dog or cat is sick, or any other disruption happened at home, they may be cranky. If there is a behaviour you can ignore and give that person more space than usual, do that. Again, this is a perfect opportunity to ask a kid from the audience, and you be the perpetrator and ask them to respond in a way to give you space. Some language to use here:

"I think they are having a tough day, maybe they need some time on their own";

or,

"We know they do not really like this game, so we shouldn't force her."

(Do a little skit here to demonstrate.)

TALK

If another student is disrupting your day and you do not like their behaviour, we encourage you to GENTLY ask the other to stop whatever they are doing. Explain that it is disrupting your day. (This teaches them to advocate for themselves by practicing in this social community we have at schools.)

SEE A TEACHER

If anything goes on that may injure another student, we ask all students to seek a teacher's help immediately. If the student has attempted to talk to another student and it did not work, they should seek a teacher's help. All staff will take the time to listen to both sides of the story. Most situations between kids can be resolved by giving the kids your undivided attention to listen to what they have to say.

This signage will reinforce how respectful behaviour towards each other creates a conducive atmosphere for learning. Everyone feels safe.

At all times staff should be modelling friendly, positive, polite behaviour.

Red Dots

(Designated Lockdown Space for Each Room in the School)

As a Principal, I present these in each classroom in a very calm, and unthreatening way. I explain they are just like the sign above the door for a fire drill. It is there to provide us with a place to go for our drills that we conduct two times a year.

Each room in the school has a designated area, identified by a six inch red dot, if there is ever a situation that calls for a lockdown. This involves having the students sit as quietly as possible if there is an armed intruder in the building. It is in the corner that has the least exposure to windows or doors in the given room.

Red dots are taped in each room, including the library, gym, and supply room. This ensures that everyone (even if there is a supply teacher) knows where to sit. Each teacher is responsible for taking their students on a school tour to show them where the red dot is in the art room, gym, computer lab, library, etc. (These are just 6" diameter fadeless paper circles.)

Samples of this Signage can be found in the attachments to this manual and available for download at www.margdodds.com.

4. Relationship Building

Why is relationship building such an important part of a principal's job?

The principal sets the tone for the building. The principal is the #1 role model. Staff, students, and parents are watching you closely all the time. The spotlight is directly on you, from the moment you enter the building until the minute you leave.

WHAT A FABULOUS OPPORTUNITY to demonstrate decorum, courtesy, politeness, and respectful behaviour towards all members of our school community. I take it as a personal challenge to make sure everyone I encounter knows to follow my lead. We emulate what we see.

Relationships are the drivers of a civil society. We begin with relationships with our parents, families, neighbours, school, and all our social groups, whether we are shopping, dancing, on a hockey team or out for a walk.

Our public schools are the only place that a child in our country is committed to for 14 years of their lives. These institutions have all kinds of rules that students must abide by because we must keep them safe.

An example of this is no snowball throwing on school yards, big areas that are covered with the fun white stuff for almost four months of the year. I am very honest with the kids and explain that if they were visiting in my backyard, we would probably have some fun throwing snow at each other, but here at school we keep the snow on the ground because my responsibility is to keep all 350-500 kids safe while out on the playground. Some activities get people too excited and then the activity goes too far, and kids get hurt. Kids understand that.

The staff hear me explain this simple rule in front of their classroom, as I do for many rules that are hard for all students to follow. The staff watch me speaking to students in the hallways in their classrooms and on yard duty all the time.

I try to model how to "banter" with the kids, instead of going outside with a police whistle and just yelling at the kids to stop swinging on the goal posts, as one example. I walk over and tell them the goal posts are slippery and two years ago a kid fell and ended up in a cast on his arm for six weeks. So please, no swinging on the goal posts. It is as important to model the way something is said as well as what is said.

Principals' relationships are being examined through a microscope by everyone, all day long. They watch how you speak to the bus drivers, care staff, teachers, educational assistants, and other students. All the while, what you are doing is building a trusting, caring community. Someday, one of these students might well be the nurse taking care of me at the old age home. I want them to be kind, compassionate, and know how to treat everyone respectfully.

Building Relationships with Staff

Office Administrator

In my experience, this is the hardest job in the building, second to the classroom teacher. Both jobs require a wide variety of skills that go well beyond their job descriptions.

The office administrator is generally the first staff member anyone meets whether over the telephone or in person at the office. They are the school's leading ambassador. Often their first conversation with a parent, student or member of the public sets the tone for all other impressions of your school. They know the families better than anyone in your building. They talk to every parent who has a child absent or sick. They serve as a counsellor who consoles both students and parents. And, they are a cheerleader for every staff member on every phone call. This person walks on water.

Custodian

The custodian either takes pride in his or her job or does not. A clean school with tidy hallways and shiny floors always sets a positive, welcoming tone! They have an important job. We need kids to use the toilets in the school for their health. A good custodian will regularly visit the bathroom to make sure the toilets are flushed. Our school is full of kids who are afraid of the noise of the flush. Good care staff are aware of this and help with regular foot flushes. (Note: If you are a new Principal, use your foot to gently flush unflushed toilets just before recess breaks. It makes a huge difference for anyone going into a clean stall.) Your custodian sets the stage for a healthy, safe and welcoming school.

Teachers

Teachers are social workers, diplomats, and and multi-taskers, from juggling teaching how to do long division to consoling Fatima because her dog died last night.

A parent missed a memo about a field trip and arrived to pick up his daughter for a dentist appointment. The parent finds out his child is on a field trip, and he must go to the Art Gallery to pick her up. He yells at the teacher because they are now going to be late. At the same time the teacher struggles to politely point out that the parent had signed the consent form but forgot which day it was.

These things happen multiple times daily to teachers whom the principal is there to support. Our job is to help them be their best selves everyday. We want their entire cup of energy focussed on their students.

I believe that the greatest support we can give these wonderful teachers is a consistent, predictable routine. For example:

- Make sure they have changes for next week's schedule in plenty of time.
- There is a Monday memo in their boxes on Friday.
- Provide lots of lead time when you expect them at meetings. A Year-long calendar with meeting dates provides them with this information.
- Identify designated meeting time for them to talk directly to teachers in their division.

These organized supports help our teachers clear the path so they can focus on the important and primary task of teaching.

Cards for All Staff

Consider creating a template to guide the ordering of cards that recognize every member of your staff such as: "Teacher's Day" (October 5th); "Administrator's Day" (February 22nd); "Welcome Back" for September; and, Christmas cards for the last day of school before the holidays (be sure to include the crossing guards, breakfast volunteers, custodians, bus drivers, and parent council volunteers). It takes me two hours to write 40 cards. The card's messages can be very brief:

- Thank you so much for always being so positive and kind when speaking to our students;
- Thank you for all you do to make our school a great place for our students;
- Wishing you a restful holiday with your family; or,
- Thank you for all your time and effort this fall helping our school get off to a fantastic start!

Once the students and staff are back in the building, your energies will be consumed by taking care of all the daily demands. Planning and organizing in advance when and how I would ensure my staff felt appreciated, alleviated huge stress. For example, I knew ahead of time that I needed two hours, on or prior to Labour Day, to write: Welcome Back Cards that would include a "voucher for one yard duty". They could use this on a day they felt too stretched to do yard duty.

You will need another hour for writing cards for International Teacher's Day (October 5th), to thank them for all their hard work ensuring a smooth start-up for students and parents. And before the last weekend of November, well before Christmas holidays, you will need to write a card wishing them well for the holidays and thanking them for their hard work in the Fall. I knew I had to have these written by November before I ran out of steam. I would simply place these cards on everyone's desk the day before the occasion or last day of classes before the break.

Additional details about these types of cards may be found
in Step 4 of the next section of this manual.

Building Relationships with Parents

Teachers and principals must use multiple skills every day because we deal with many unpredictable issues. This happens when you are dealing with large groups of people in any organization.

Schools have children in their care for a **HUGE** amount of time. Every parent wants the best for their child. If the parent is concerned about the way the school is caring for their child, the issue needs to be addressed immediately.

Children have a sixth sense. They know if there is tension at home between parents, and this also holds true for tension between school, caregivers and parents. The child needs to feel safe, calm, and relaxed for optimal learning. We have evidence of this through the National Council on Teacher Quality research. If a child feels torn between their parent and their school, they will not relax enough to learn. They will be pre-occupied on watching for any issues or perceived mis-steps they have heard their parent complain about. This puts a huge amount of stress on the student who is trying to learn.

This stress often manifests itself in the child's body by producing cortisol, a stress hormone, that controls mood, motivation, and fear - without them understanding the huge effect on their bodies. Cortisol shoots into their systems without them understanding that their bodies are having a chemical reaction. The reaction wreaks havoc on young kids. They feel anxiety that they are not able to explain or comprehend. They just know that they are discombobulated and unhappy.

A continued state of anxiety soon creates situations that embarrasses the youngster and deepens the anxiety. (An example of this would be a young child wetting their pants. This is devastating for a four or five year-old, even when we play down the incident as much as possible.) If a child is anxious, their tummies may tighten up and they cannot eat their lunch. An hour or so later, they have an uncharacteristic tantrum caused by low blood sugar. They do not understand. They just know they feel miserable about being at school, which exacerbates the initial issue.

These invisible stresses can result in much bigger problems if not dealt with at the onset of these behaviors. Parents and teachers need to work together so the child understands that everyone is on the same team and wants the best for them.

It is very important to tackle any issues causing a child to be afraid or hesitant to come to school. The quicker these issues are resolved, the better for the student. You want to prevent the problem from growing to a point it becomes far more difficult to address.

Trusting relationships with parents is the only way to make sure that all the children in your care are getting the most out of each day they are with you.

Parents must trust that we are going to do our very best for their children. This relationship is so very important. Dustups with parents must be addressed immediately. Angry parents impact their child's learning in ways they can't imagine.

You want the students and their parents saying positive things about your school when they head home. If a parent is angry or upset with the school, this will transfer to the child. The child will feel like you don't have their back and will be sitting in a classroom with so much anxiety in their brain that the cerebral cortex can't function properly.

Most often, the parent needs to communicate directly with you. **MAKE THE TIME**. After the parent has said everything they need to say, ask if you can have a day to come up with a solution to the issue and either call them or arrange a face-to- face meeting or phone call. You need the time to hear the other side of the story and a clear picture of what has happened. If the issue is not resolved, the one suffering is the student, who feels pulled between the parent and authority figure in the school. It may be an issue with the teacher, lunch hour assistant, bus driver, another student, or an educational assistant. Whatever it is, it cannot wait because the child you are there to serve will get pulled further and further away from a trusting relationship at school.

Building Relationships with Students

We are here to provide each child with the opportunity to reach their most richly desired dreams. It is incumbent for us to create optimal learning environments.

As you will read further on, *Elementary Teachers Federation of Ontario* produced a study that showed how vital relationships are for optimal learning. An example was teachers who took two minutes a day for 10 consecutive days for an unstructured conversation (in the hallway, at lunch, while on yard duty, or walking to the bus) with a student who was struggling or disruptive. Results showed that a student's trajectory for success could be improved by 85%. Is it difficult for teachers to find those two minutes a day for 10 consecutive days? ABSOLUTELY. However, the result is indisputable and makes the time investment worthwhile.

The students we traditionally invest more time in are those who are usually challenging. Their names often come up and are discussed at divisional in-school meetings every month. There are usually mitigating circumstances that weigh heavy on these kids. I encourage and support the teacher taking the approach described above for two weeks. Once they have tried it, the proof is in the pudding. They will do it over and over and encourage colleagues to do it because the results make their entire classroom and year run more smoothly.

It only takes one student to disrupt an entire class. Good teachers with excellent classroom management know this and target relationship building with the most disruptive kids first. This allows them the most productivity out of their students for the 6.5 hours we have with them each day.

I had an opportunity to work with a vice-principal who also taught Grade 8. He came to me the week before school started and asked me if I could cover his class for 40 minutes a day for the first three weeks of school. This was an unusual request. He explained t3hat being new to the school community he wanted to have 20-minute interviews with each of his students. He had a series of questions about things they felt talented at, what they preferred to do in leisure time, and whether there was anything they were concerned or worried about for their last year of elementary school. (Note: This list of questions is available on the website.)

I thought this was absolutely brilliant. We sorted out how we were going to cover his class while he spent this time with each and every student. By Thanksgiving, he had absolute trust from all his students, and they were not afraid to take risks. Giving students uninterrupted time to express themselves to an adult is the most powerful tool we have for students to feel valued in their school community.

This is also true for family situations. Listening is a lost art. Listening gives the child an opportunity to know that their voice is heard and valued. In any of our relationships, we will take more risks once we know we can trust and get support from those around us. This positive impact is further magnified in a school situation.

We ask students to put forth their best efforts and produce products in all kinds of areas. Of course, we all have our strengths, weaknesses, and dominant learning style (VARK: Visual, Auditory, Reading/Writing, and Kinesthetic). A brilliant reader is asked by their teacher to produce work in seven other subject areas each day. There is no other time in our lives that we are expected to produce so many tasks that are then going to be judged.

Starting School: Kindergarten

When children enter kindergarten, it is often their first experience in a large group environment that is organized, structured, where they are expected to follow a set of uniform rules. They find themselves taken from the security of their home and parents for 6.5 hours a day! It is a completely different experience than playing with a small group at home or daycare setting. During the first week of school, they are thrust into this new environment, where they need to trust that these strangers (staff) will help and care for them as they navigate their day.

This first month of school for a JK is probably the steepest learning curve they will encounter in their entire school experience. Self-regulation learned during this month will set them up for social order for the rest of their lives. Learning how to share and wait for the adult to deal with their concern is one example. At home, a parent or caregiver can immediately deal with issues as they arise. In a school setting, the child may need to wait three to five minutes for their teacher's attention. This is an eternity for a four-year-old child.

For example: Going to the bathroom. They find out that they have to tell a teacher when they need to go to the bathroom. For some this may be very strange. It may have only been a year earlier when they first proudly accomplished being able to go on their own. And now they must ask to go! What's up with that?

It is an understandable, challenging, and confusing time for these youngsters. Being in a large group with strange new faces with rules and structure may make some feel insecure and unsafe. The most important thing for a child to be in an environment where they can feel SAFE so that they can learn and absorb information.

5. Communication

Regular, consistent communication between school and home is imperative. It ensures positive relationships between each child's parents/guardians and individual teachers. This creates a safety blanket for the child. For this reason, keeping the lines of communication open and frequent is key. Tools such as an annual calendar facilitate regular contact and communication. Parents can see when parent council meetings, family dances, end of month assemblies, and the Remembrance Day Assemblies are held, all of which they are invited to attend.

Parents have a major influence on children's well-being. Holding monthly social activities, where parents can wander through their child's classroom and throughout the school, creates opportunities for informal communication.

Another example is having teachers make one positive phone call per month per student. This may also sound daunting, but only takes a couple of minutes. A teacher can choose to do two per day on their release time, after school or in the evening when they know the child will be there to hear this praise.

Remember, self-esteem/confidence is the number one driver in success and applies to parents too! After a while, the parent will see the call from the school on their phone and won't have an anxiety attack because they think their child is physically injured (the #1 reason schools call home) or their child is in trouble (the #2 reason).

Parents will quickly learn to understand that we all want the very best for their child. When there are issues (there will be lots), and a parent comes to speak with a teacher or principal (for a whole variety of reasons), it will no longer feels confrontational. We will all know we are working together on a solution to the problem.

Student Agendas

Keeping parents informed can also be facilitated by the structured use of the agendas provided to each student. Keeping an agenda is a huge life skill. Teachers can use this tool to inform parents of things coming up for the month. They may use a writing class to direct the students on how to fill in the monthly calendar and use colours for assignment due dates, field trips, or student-led-conference days. Doing this monthly as a group really helps all children to develop this skill. It can help students to anticipate and get enthused about upcoming events. It also teaches them how to manage their time themselves to effectively complete assignments on time.

Some of the teachers simply use a happy face sticker to let parents know that all went well that day. Others may take the time to write a comment in each agenda. Some will have the students write their own comment for the day to have parents' sign. The sky's the limit. Inexperienced teachers will learn how important it is to have positive relationships with the parents when the tough stuff comes along. Of course, working with 28-30 kids in a classroom, the tough stuff will come along.

Staff Communications Plan

Establish a staff communications plan before the start of the year. This will include all staff meetings, in-school divisional meetings, and parent nights/conferences. Communication is the fundamental building block for all relationships. Having the road map laid out for all staff demonstrates your commitment to good communication. Each interest group in your building craves time to talk directly with you. By establishing these opportunities, you will help eliminate the lineups at your door at the end of the school day. For example, the staff member from Grade 3 knows that he is going to have the opportunity to discuss his concern at an uninterrupted meeting on Thursday.

I believe that having built-in opportunities for communication helps to support the staff who are working so hard to help the future generation of tomorrow.

Staff need to know that the principal is always available to confide in when issues arise between staff, students, or anything else that causes frustration or anger. These issues deplete the staff member's energy, which means that not 100% of their energy is spent on the students in their care. The principal's role is to clear any big rocks out of the teachers' path that might deplete their energy. The principal's door should remain open unless there is a confidential phone call or meeting. This is much harder than it seems, but it is essential for walking the talk of being a welcoming, nurturing leader. Remember, you are the number one role model for everyone else in your building.

Further details about student agendas and staff communications are described in Steps 1 - 4 found in the next section of this manual.

6. The Importance of Structure

A school building is filled with zillions of moving pieces. As the principal of the building, we establish and maintain a foundation, environment, and framework where everyone is able to thrive. The foundation needs to be as strong as possible so that students, staff, and caregivers understand their roles and expectations. The school environment needs to be positive, energetic, and collaborative. And the operating framework needs to be simple, consistent, well communicated and understood.

We have staff who feel confident and staff who are overwhelmed. We have students ranging from 3.5 years old (just babies) to 14-year-olds adolescents (who find themselves experiencing rapid physical, cognitive and psycho-social change, who are not always in the emotional driver's seat, and who may truly have no understanding that they are not in control). All these people have an array of emotions, frustrations, and responsibilities.

A school is like an organism. If each part is functioning optimally, it is healthy, and things run smoothly. As soon as one piece goes out of kilter, it affects the entire organism. Like a broken spoke on a wheel, it will keep turning until the pressure is too much on the other spokes and one by one, they snap.

Our staff includes Lunch Hour Assistants (minding the students while they eat), bus drivers who need to be courteous to the students while they are transported to and from home, teachers who need to provide exciting, engaging curriculum and the custodian, who keeps the school clean – creating a nice atmosphere. Students need to be responsible for clearing up after themselves and placing their boots along the wall in an orderly fashion so the care staff can wipe up the water melting from their snow boots following a recess.

Having a structure that everyone is aware of, understands and follows, gives each part of the organism the best chance for optimal health. Without structure and expectations laid out explicitly for staff, considerable miscommunication can happen. When you are dealing with so many people, miscommunication can result in problems that could have been dealt with proactively and not reactively. The amount of energy used in a proactive situation is much less than the energy spent reacting. When we are reacting, we become anxious, angry, and frustrated, which floods our brains with a fight or flight response. Not even aware of what is happening, we react from a place that cannot access the best part of our brain to come up with a solution.

Always give yourself time to calm down as soon as you are aware that your stomach is tight (in a knot). Your body is telling you to slow down and calm down so you can **literally think clearly**.

A structured, well-planned year eases everyone's stress levels in countless ways. From knowing what is expected as a staff member, to students knowing when their routines will be interrupted – structure helps set up everyone in the building for a positive experience.

If staff have children to get home to or other commitments, a pre-planned calendar lets them know well in advance when they need to make other arrangements. Their participation in meetings is crucial. The agenda for meetings should consist of the issues that cannot be dealt with in a simple memo or email. Everyone's time is their most valuable resource. It is up to the principal to demonstrate that not a minute should be wasted. By having all staff committed to these pre-arranged times, many of the issues that cause frustration can be eliminated. With so many staff juggling so many balls, the best we can do is give them a solid foundation and great communication tools to work with.

7. Success Measures

The success of a school is data informed. We also know that the measures of a school's success are not limited to academic measures. There are a number of indirect and related factors that a principal needs to consider.

Student Attendance

The first piece of data is student attendance. If kids are not at school, they are not in a position for success. Kids must be happy to go to school for optimal achievement.

Although there are provincial laws about attendance, they are difficult to enforce. Missing one day a week amounts to two months of the school year. A student cannot possibly catch up. We have students with health conditions that prohibit them from attending. Every effort is made to help them keep up with the class by having the school board provide a tutor. Predictably, children lose their self-confidence when they fall behind.

In some homes, school is not held in high regard. Parents who struggled in school and did not have positive experiences may need time to build trust with the school their children are attending. An extreme example of this are families who have been directly or indirectly impacted by the residential school system. They, understandably, have a lack of trust in the idea that school as a safe place. Sensitivity to the cultural and socio-economic welfare of a student's family or school community needs to be considered. These may require specific strategies to address.

Staff Attendance

Staff attendance predicts how well the school will operate. In well-oiled schools, there is less sickness amongst staff, fewer mental health issues, and less stress leave. Superintendents know which schools are struggling by looking at staff absenteeism.

People who are happy when they come to work are much more productive. Feeling appreciated makes us work harder. Staff who have their talents are celebrated are more likely to do extra. We are well aware of all the expectations of our teachers. They need our encouragement and praise.

Healthy School Committee

A very effective approach to both assessing and improving student success is by the principal establishing a Healthy School Committee. The purpose of the Committee is to have a direct communication with the Principal to make suggestions to improve the school atmosphere. I established this Committee early on as a Principal and found them to be remarkably successful in gaining insight about the functioning of the school from a student's perspective.

This Committee is organized by the principal. I would go into each class, explain what the Committee is all about and ask for two student volunteers (from classes Grade 3 and up) to participate. If more expressed interest in joining, I always said YES! I would explain that the volunteers would need to give one recess a month to participate. The students would meet in the library over a lunch/recess period once per month. They would sit in a circle and each student would get to comment on the five areas of the school (Environment, Healthy Eating, Safety, Physical Fitness, and Any Other Concerns).

Each student takes a turn commenting on the topic. Some have concerns and others will say 'pass'. As we go around the circle, inevitably an idea will come to a kid who has already had their turn. Each student has a piece of paper and pencil to write their ideas down their ideas before they forget them. Then we go around the circle again. This saves so much time as it removes interruptions. Each student knows that they have the opportunity to speak to me directly once a month at these meetings. It opens a direct line of communication between the front line (the students) and the lead teacher (principal) who is in a position to make changes and accommodations, if necessary.

I was able to invite our school nurse from the local health unit to attend the monthly meetings. This helped enhance both the student's sense of Committee's importance and school's interest in what they had to say.

Attendance at Healthy School Committee meetings will indicate very quickly to you whether the students feel their time is valued. It is a good indicator of what is on a student's mind and often includes concerns that the adults have not considered.

Step 2 in the next section of this manual provides further information.

Parent Council Meetings

Participation in Parent Meetings is another measure of how your school is doing. Letting parents know that they are welcome and that there is a structured forum for them to openly discuss concerns or suggestions is a direct accountability tool. If there are fractious issues to discuss, please give yourself time to get back to the parents. When an issue arises be sure to say: "Thank you for bringing this to my attention. I will address your concerns as soon as possible and get back to you."

Student Achievement

Finally, the largest measure of success is student achievement. Schools with high student and staff absenteeism, that have chaotic hallways and disruptive classrooms, do not have the kind of environment required for students to achieve their potential. Student achievement is the driver of everything else that happens in your building. Student achievement is measured academically, but character development is crucial as well.

We are living in the 21st century. In the last 25 years, we have learned that academic success is not the best predictor of success later in life. We know that while we must set high expectations for academic skills, we must also place as much emphasis on emotional intelligence. The Wall Street Journal reports that the top four in-demand skills are communication, collaboration, leadership, and time management.

This is where self-esteem and confidence win the race. We help our students to grow self-esteem and confidence by teaching them resilience, perseverance, conscientiousness, compassion, curiosity, creativity and responsibility for their own words and actions. The development of character attributes can also be measured simply through checklists the kids complete in their classrooms monthly.

Here in Ontario, individual results of our Education Quality and Accountability Office (EQAO) standardized student tests, inform teachers where their teaching has been successful as well as areas they need to work on. There are many debates about standardized testing and its expense. I have not come up with an alternative that measures student progress in such a precise way. The individual results give the teachers a clear picture of where students need more help. The principal needs to provide time for the teachers to examine these results by division so that we can tackle our teaching strategies and areas of growth as a team. The information we gain from such tests provide professional growth opportunities.

8. Importance of a Mentor/Confidant

At my first meeting with fellow principals from my region, I passed a blank piece of paper around and asked my colleagues to write five things they wished they'd known when they started this job. I read through the list and discovered many things I would not have thought of. I know I avoided many issues by listening to those with experience.

I was also lucky enough to be matched with a mentor. If your board has an established mentorship program, take advantage of it. If not, seek out a person you admire and approach them. Scheduling an early breakfast or dinner once every six weeks seems to be manageable for most. **THESE NEED TO BE TREATED LIKE SPECIALIST DOCTOR APPOINTMENTS.**

My mentor and I quickly realized that our respective school days were so long and busy that we needed to treat our mentor meetings like they were doctor's appointments. We agreed to dinner once every six weeks! Sitting down for 1.5 hours can clear up so many queries that it is well worth the time.

I learned several things from exemplary principals that I wanted to share with my staff. Of course, I also learned a lot of things from previous principals that I would never do to staff.

As administrators, we make up to 200 decisions every day that affect others. Having a trusted colleague with whom to discuss daunting or sensitive issues will save you the need for counselling appointments. This is a **BIG** job you are stepping into. So much of what we do is confidential. It is essential that you have a confidant, particularly when disturbing incidents happen in your school community.

Throughout my career, I regularly attended conferences and read all kinds of books on leadership, how to be a great principal, and how to get the best out of your teaching staff. I then began to implement the strategies that resonated most.

After I retired and was temporarily hired to support some schools, I realized that I had developed a school management system for principals would work for any principal. I decided that it was worth sharing with other school administrators.

There is no magic wand. But there are foundational steps to follow in order to put your staff in a position to help their students succeed. It is all about making sure each kid feels safe, happy, and confident. The steps outlined in this book will help to ensure that your staff, students (and their parents) all feel this way about your school.

9. You Can Do This

You have the ability, the organizational skills, and the enthusiasm to make your school one that every staff member wants to work at, every student feels welcome and wants to attend, and every parent is happy their child has you as a role model.

You will ooze positivity. You make everyone you encounter in a day feel a little bit brighter!

Put on your invincibility cloak every morning to help you get through every crisis, emergency and all the decisions you make in a day (apparently up to 200), with ease because you have a staff that feels great coming to work and who know they are appreciated. You have cleared the path for them to focus on teaching. These strategies will motivate your staff to come to work and give it their best.

**YOUR STAFF WILL BE THE
OUTSTANDING ROLE MODELS
YOU WANT THEM
TO BE FOR ALL THE CHILDREN IN YOUR CARE
AND AS A RESULT,
YOUR STUDENTS WILL THRIVE!**

SECTION TWO

HERE WE GO!!!!

One simple step at a time:

Your practical guide to

lead a

THRIVING SCHOOL!!!

Setting the Stage for a Firm Foundation

Set yourself up for success before the year begins. With the following activities completed before the school year starts, every staff member knows what is expected and the school year will get off on the right foot.

1. Tour Your School – Have lots of positive signage up on the walls. Every nationality in your school should be represented in the posters, murals, and signage you have up on the walls in your welcoming school building.

2. Have a road map for all "investors" in your school building in the form of a year-long calendar. All holidays, professional development days, regular staff meetings, in-school meetings, Professional Learning Community and Parent Meetings are all set before school starts and everyone knows when they need to be available.

3. Have your Staff Handbook ready for your first PD Day or Staff Meeting. If this is not occurring until after the first day with children you will NEED to ask them to have their first staff meeting on the second day of school. (Bring good munchies with you).

4. Have your Tuesday Folders and Family Handbooks ready to go home for the first day of school. This gets everyone off to a great start!

This section of the manual describes a four-step process that sets the stage for the school year, establishes the foundation and framework for success, along with creating the environment for the school to thrive.

STEP 1: Building the School Year Framework

School Calendar

I have included a September 2022 to June 2023 calendar on the website. You can just add, change or delete anything on the calendar that does not suit your school. This includes staff meetings once per month, Principals' meetings, and In-School monthly divisional meetings. Your staff needs to know where you are at all times. If you are out of the building and your Vice-Principal is taking your place, or if there is a teacher in-charge, your entire staff needs to know who that person is in case of emergency. Emergencies do not arise when we have time for them!

This simple gesture of communication will take stress off your staff knowing they have support at all times while they are in the school building. This helps establish a circle of trust. It also helps demonstrate your transparent management approach.

Setting out the dates for your staff meetings lets every staff member know the days they need to arrange for after-school care for their children, and to rearrange doctor and dentist appointments. You want everyone in attendance at these important meetings, so you need to set expectations up front to avoid misunderstandings. Memos and emails cannot replace the "vibes" you get from in-person staff meetings. This allows you to check-in with everyone and make sure nothing is going off the rails. Being proactive saves immeasurable time and energy if you nip problems in the bud.

The calendar needs to be large and prominently displayed in a central location like a front foyer. By large, I mean each month presented on a piece of Bristol board. Persons passing by the calendar will start taking a minute to check it out. It will take up to 4 months for staff to get used to the idea that you would like them to help keep this visible calendar updated by writing directly on it. Eventually they will start adding things like sports practices or club meetings. Parents coming in and out of the school will also start checking it for upcoming events and activities.

This calendar is the same one that is included at the end of the family and staff handbooks. Any tweaks, additions, or changes will be sent out as the last page of the Monthly Newsletter. The calendar will always be a work in progress and should be adjusted when necessary. PARENTS LOVE IT. It helps them to organize their home calendars when they know well in advance of Professional Development Days, holidays, and days you are hoping they can come to the school.

In the enclosed year-long calendar, I embed bi-monthly invitations to participate in school activities. I know this sounds daunting, but it really is no extra work. Simply pick a specific colour that means "parents included" on your calendar. As you can see in the sample calendar included at the end of this manual and in colour on the website, events and activities like:

- Welcome Back Classroom Visits
- End of Month Assemblies
- Student-Led Conferences
- End of Year Barbeque
- Family Dance Nights

- Holiday Concert
- Science Fair
- Family Math Night
- Board Game Night
- or even a Poetry Café

are all included. The sky's the limit.

I have never seen an electronic calendar work as well as sending each family a hard copy. Trust me on this. This simple concept has many ripple effects. It shows your staff you are committed to the meetings you set.

A 2022-23 School Calendar Template is available at the backend of the manual and for download at www.margdodds.com.

Staff Handbook

The purpose of the Staff Handbook is to provide the school's policies, procedures, and protocols. It should provide clear guidance and direction to staff and what is expected of them. There must be constant supervision of the students in your care. It must be clear who is responsible for them at each minute of the day. This will eliminate many preventable issues.

We all wish that we could hand out the Staff Handbook and count on everyone to sit down and read it. **THIS DOES NOT WORK**. At your first meeting, whether it's before students start school or once classes have begun, provide a really good treat for staff and sit down with them and go through it page by page. IT DOES NOT HAVE TO BE A PAINFUL EXPERIENCE. Returning staff will groan about it (that is why you have good food).

TAKE THE TIME TO GO THROUGH YOUR HANDBOOK PAGE BY PAGE, RIGHT AT THE BEGINNING OF THE YEAR.

This step is key to ensuring that everyone understands what is expected of them every day. It clarifies your expectations regarding how to engage with each other and what must be accomplished. When one or two do not pull their weight on the team, it can undermine the climate of the whole school. That's why clarity is essential.

Once you have taken everyone's time to review your expectations, it makes it easier to speak to staff the first time they are late in greeting their students at the classroom door, yard duty, forgetting it was their week to clear the halls for bus dismissal, and the list goes on.

When one, two or three people have a misstep, **PLEASE** go and speak to them directly. Avoid the trap of putting a reminder on the Monday Memo to all staff, most of whom are doing their best and do not need to feel as though they are guilty of the crime. Also, not everyone needs to be reminded during a staff meeting. It is uncomfortable. And the teacher who has missed something needs to be held accountable for whatever it was. **GO DIRECTLY TO THE INDIVIDUAL** to speak to them.

As the principal in the building, one way to ensure your staff is consistently implementing the key protocols, is to be visible in the hallways. All the while each of your staff is role modelling courteous and respectful conversations with colleagues and students. Our students watch us all the time. (They will tell you if you lost an earring before you know it is gone.)

Talk to your office staff and explain that you do not want any parent meetings or phone calls during the 20 minutes when students enter the school in the morning, or at dismissal at the end of the day. You want to check that all staff are in the hallways, supervising their students, offering greetings in the morning, and wishing them a happy evening as they go out the door at the end of the day. This gesture has a HUGE impact on how staff, students, and parents feel about the school day. It is not rocket science but is essential for growing positive relationships. Remember: Our students are constantly observing us all the time.

The handbook should also outline how staff will work together to keep everything organized and tidy, from the gym closet with all the equipment and the staff room to the supply cupboard with art supplies and the library. These housekeeping issues are easily resolved if you are proactive. Without these simple steps, a lot of chaos can ensue. This wastes the teachers' precious energy, which we want to save for the kids. Remember, we should aim to have 100% of each teacher's and EA's energy spent on children, not on avoidable frustrations.

Your school will already have a handbook. Compare it to the sample handbook template provided in this book. You may wish to tweak yours and align it with your own preferences accordingly.

When there is a clear understanding of the handbook, the entire staff will keep up to the standard of decorum we strive for.

It will relieve so many little issues that can undermine staff morale. We must free up as much time as possible to continuously lift-up our staff so they can shine!

A Sample Staff Handbook Template is available at the backend of the manual and for download at www.margdodds.com.

Family Handbook

All relevant and key information related to the school, its operations, protocols, the responsibilities of parents, students, teachers, and other staff are described in this document. The handbook also contains the year-long calendar. The family handbook provides a great opportunity to position your school as the most welcoming one your students and parents have ever experienced.

On the first day of school, send a copy home with the youngest in the family. (My experience shows that it gets into the parents' hands if the youngest one takes it.) The handbook covers all the school's housekeeping items. You will always have new students you were not expecting in September, so it handy have 30 extra copies on hand.

As families move in throughout the year, office staff can give a copy to the guardian or parent. It will relieve a lot of stress for the incoming family. It also will answer many questions the parent may not have thought to ask during the 'Welcome to our School' tour. A Grade 8 Ambassador has the job of giving new families a tour of the school. The handbook clearly outlines expectations we have of the students at school, on the playground, bus rides, during recess and excursions. When the inevitable happens, it is very easy to explain to the child and their parents the misstep and consequences.

Each classroom teacher is asked to go through the section that deals with behavior with their class on the first day of school. Again, clear expectations and consequences help everyone to know what the boundaries are. Depending how large your school is, many of us deal with an average of 300 students and 30 to 40 staff members. Clear expectations help everyone to be successful.

A Sample Family Handbook Template is available is available at the end of the manual and for download at www.margdodds.com.

Monday Memos

Each **Friday** morning, the staff should receive a "Monday Memo" from you (sent via email along with a hard copy in their mailboxes). This is simply an update for the following week, with all the items already on your calendar with any changes or additions from Monday to Friday. We know most staff do a lot of their planning and set up for the following week on weekends. To help them be proactive with their planning, they need to know which days they may be interrupted by special assemblies, visits from the Fire Department, safety drills (such as fire), and lock down drills.

All teachers must be given time to prepare their students when there is an anticipated change to their daily routine. For example: If a fire alarm rings for an expected drill, those with noise sensitivity (e.g., those with autism) must be given their earmuffs ahead of time, an EA can prepare them.

We cannot have students miss out on activities simply because they were unaware of, not prepared, or unable to cope with the changes. For example, missing gym because it is being used for an assembly or as a polling station. At any time, and there will be many, when there is a change in routine or interruptions in the day, we need to do our best to let everyone know ahead of time to prepare themselves. The more time we can give staff to prepare their class for these interruptions (and sometimes disappointments), the better.

If each staff member has the following weeks' Monday Memo on Friday, there will be no surprises that cause unnecessary stress in the building.

> *A Sample 'Monday Memo' is available is available at the end of the manual and for download at www.margdodds.com.*

Tuesday Folders

Trust me here. During my first year as a principal, one of my teaching colleagues shared a very successful idea at a staff meeting. A colleague from another school had started sending home Tuesday Folders. Each folder had two pockets. One said "Please keep at home"; the other said, "Thank you for returning this to school."

Anything coming from the office was sent home in this folder. Monthly Newsletters (with updated calendars on the back page), permission slips for field trips, inoculations from Health Unit, extra-curricular teams or clubs starting up. Eventually, all staff began including all information for parents in the same folder.

It may sound a little overwhelming, BUT IT WORKS. Here is how. Have your Admin Assistant generate a template of 2" X 4" labels with:

- "Please keep at home"
- "Thank you for returning to school"
- A class list (In June)

Have the Admin Assistant also make labels for each folder, e.g., *Student Name, Tuesday Folder.*

Then, in early June, ask four responsible Grade 7's for their help. Each student gets a pile of the same-coloured Tuesday Folders that hopefully match your School Colours. Each folder will have "Please keep at home" on the right-hand side and *"Thank you for returning this to school"* on the left-hand side.

They will each have 100 folders (or more, depending on your student population). Then the office administrator gives them the labels for individual students in their next year's classroom. (You should have these sorted out by mid-June when you are figuring out your classes and teacher needs for the following school year.) Get them sorted now while you have Grade 7 and 8 students to help you.

These folders need to have all the registration sheets in them that are sent home the first day of school, with changes of addresses, emergency contacts and so on.

Your office administrator will also generate a class list with the youngest in the family highlighted for each classroom teacher and Educational Assistants for their classrooms. The youngest in the family will have the one family copy of the school handbook. These students will also be the ones to receive all material that is for the school population and multiple copies are not necessary. (Monthly newsletters should also be sent electronically.)

Parents will learn to check their child's backpack on Tuesdays for information coming from the school. Newsletters and other information where only one copy is needed for each family goes home with the youngest in the family. Parents get in the routine of having change on hand for pizza days or for book sales.

Parents of all grades will also come to realize that they only need to dig through their child's backpack once per week for the Folder.

Informative Monthly Newsletters

The School Newsletter is sent home at the beginning of each month. It includes character education (one attribute or grandfather teaching/month). The Seven Grandfather Teachings are a set of traditional First Nation teachings on conduct towards each other to ensure peaceful, supportive communities. They are Wisdom, Love, Respect, Truth, Honesty, Humility, and Bravery. All of us want each student to develop into a caring, compassionate, and responsible citizen. This needs to be encouraged.

The newsletter is easiest for all if you use the same template each month. A list of monthly Birthdays on the front page is well received by staff and students! The newsletter should also include a language, math, and healthy habit suggestion. All changes to the calendar and all other school community events for the month are on the back page of the newsletter.

A Sample Newsletter is available is available at the end of the manual and for download at www.margdodds.com.

Resolving an Issue

Students will be sent to you during the day and often during lunch and recess periods for inappropriate action or behaviour. They are likely emotional and their adrenaline is pumping. They may have they just done something physical with another child outside. When dealing with such a situation, PLEASE, never raise your voice. As soon as you do, the garage door slams shut, the kid shuts down too, and they will not communicate effectively.

Barbara Coloroso, author of many teaching and parenting books, advocated giving all parties involved at least 10 minutes to calm down, sometimes longer. Have juice boxes, granola bars or water bottles available in your office. The kids often have low blood sugar when infractions occur. Sit eye to eye with the child and REALLY listen. Once you've done that, they can usually come up with their own solution. This only works if you give them space and time to calm themselves.

The next step is to ask any other students who were DIRECTLY involved (not witnesses) to join the two of you and have them tell their side of the story. Explain that each member of the circle will have a chance to respond, but that we need to listen without interrupting while each person explains their side of the story.

In any school, the same five or six students are usually repeat offenders.

Self-regulation for those students is REALLY HARD. We need to teach life skills here. Treat each student with gentleness and compassion. Almost without exception, once everyone has had their chance to be heard, the kids will figure out for themselves what the solution and the consequences should be. We know that punitive measures do not work. Thousands of researchers have told us this for decades. There may need to be a suspension for one student hurting another or perhaps some recess detentions. The kids will already know this. All these rules are clearly laid out in the Family Handbook.

STEP 2: Ensure All Interest Groups in the Building have Designated Time for Your Undivided Attention (Staff, Students, and Parents)

I do not know of any other profession that manages the number of "interest groups" and variety of issues, at the same time, on a daily basis.

GOOD FOR YOU!

By establishing these meetings on your calendar, you will have designated time to discuss concerns with all the school community stakeholders. The teachers will have the opportunity to discuss any of their classroom concerns on a regular, ongoing basis at the In-School meetings.

You will also have established:

- an opportunity for students to express their suggestions or concerns at Healthy School Meetings;
- organized weekly meetings with your Lunch Hour Assistants; and,
- you will have six invitations for parents to meet with you for any of their concerns or suggestions.

These designated meetings are proactive and will help you to resolve issues before they have a chance to snowball.

In-School Meetings

In-school Meetings are monthly meetings of teachers by division. (Primary JK-3, Junior Grade 4-6, Intermediate Grade7 and 8.) Optimally, all teachers who interact with the students of that division are in attendance.

The Special Education teacher and the French/Ojibway teachers are asked to attend all three meetings. This is a huge demand on their time. To help mitigate this issue I provide a supply teacher for them to have preparation time for .5 day every 6 weeks.

The classroom teachers, principal and vice-principal are always in attendance.

The purpose for these meetings is for small groups to be able to discuss any issues they are having in their classrooms. It provides opportunity for staff members to seek their colleagues' advice with challenges they are having. You can start the discussion in the order of Grade from youngest to oldest this month, and next month, reverse the order, starting from oldest to youngest.

Each teacher has the chance to raise one concern at a time. In the past we have literally gone around the table and given everyone a chance to respond to how they have addressed a similar situation in the past, or how they may try to resolve the problem in the future. The best outcome from these supportive talks is that everyone begins to feel like they are supported by the team. No one is in it alone. When certain student names arise from the discussion you will find that each teacher in the hallway or on duty will reach out to those students with a quick hello or a chat.

By the second month of these meetings, no one will be late or not able to attend. Each classroom teacher, language, educational assistant, or special education teacher wants to approach delicate student situations as a united front with the best outcome for the student top of mind. In my experience, these meetings are invaluable. It enables us to know what the issues are in each other's classrooms. Listening to issues from their colleagues is a wonderful and worthwhile communication opportunity.

Healthy School Committee Meetings

No one knows the school like the students. Once a month, invite two students from each Grade 4 to 8 classroom, who have volunteered to be their class representatives, to have their lunch with you (in the library or an available room). Set the tables up so that everyone is sitting in a circle. There are six agenda items: Physical Activity, Healthy Eating, Safe Physical Environment, Bullying, and Healthy Message Bulletin Board. (Grade 7 and 8 has the responsibility of changing this bulletin board once a month.)

Give each student a chance to share their concerns and suggestions with you. It will take a couple of meetings until they feel that you are really listening. Once that happens, you will learn about so many issues that were previously invisible to you. Examples include:

- a need for more soccer nets at recess so other grades can play, while the Grades 7/8 use the permanent soccer goals on the playground;
- the need for toilet paper in the boys' bathroom;
- a problem on the school bus that has not been brought to your attention.

Giving students structured time to communicate issues from their classmates is such a wonderful communication opportunity. Things that bother the kids can be solved if we know about them.

These take 40 minutes, once a month. Being proactive solves many issues before they get bigger. Each student learns that we will go around the table, and everyone will have a chance to contribute. They can pass if they have nothing to say about the topic we are on. Each topic goes around the table two or three times. As the kids listen to each other, it stimulates more ideas, so you need to give everyone a chance to respond. The dates for these meetings should be scheduled to avoid conflicts like choir practice or volleyball practice. Teachers know that one recess with these students is an important meeting. Any staff is welcome to join as well if they are interested. I make it a priority to always attend and listen to their concerns.

Parent Council Meetings for Open Communication

Invite parents to six meetings throughout the year. It is often a time parents feel comfortable asking questions about upcoming events, changes in staffing, and providing suggestions on how things might run more smoothly. I always enjoyed these meetings. Parents have insights about their child's experience. There are often simple solutions to issues we were not aware of.

I know that meeting parents can be intimidating. We must put every effort forward to create strong lines of communication between the school and home.

Clearly communicate that these meetings are intended for matters concerning the school and not for questions about individual students. Sending out an agenda ahead of time is also helpful. For example:

- Welcome and Introductions
- New Business (Anything coming up in the month ahead)
- Principal's report (A chance to share all the wonderful things that have happened in the building the past month)
- Suggestions/Concerns,
- General Information (Remind all of the next meeting time that has already been established.)

Provide a snack. These meetings are scheduled from 6:00-7:00, so you can be home by 7:30 and ready for the next day.

Rotation and Meetings with Lunch Hour Assistants

I invite the Lunch Hour Assistants (LHA) to the first Assembly and introduce each of them to all the students. I present each LHA a NEW bright orange vest to wear so children can easily identify them when they are spread out on the playground. (I also provide each staff member with a safety vest, so everyone knows who is on supervision duty.)

It is common to have Lunch Hour Assistants supervise students outside at recess. Each assistant should be given the opportunity to work with all the students, so when they are outside with everyone running in different directions, they can speak to each child by name. Rotate the assistants every week. It normally takes until the end of October for them to know everyone.

Meet with these assistants once per week. Ten minutes before the first nutrition break on Tuesdays worked for me. I would ask if they had any concerns. This helped us to deal with any issues in a proactive manner. This practice enables you to find out if problems are emerging, such as disrespectful students who aren't listening to the Lunch Hour Assistant (LHA).

If any student is disrespectful to the Lunch Hour Assistant, I simply invite the student who did not take the Lunch Hour Assistant's direction to have a meeting with him or her. I have the LHA listen to the child's side of the story and then have the child listen to the LHA side. Once they speak to each other directly, most problems are resolved. MAKING TIME TO LISTEN TO BOTH SIDES IS ESSENTIAL. This is done prior to the lunch immediately following the infraction. The LHA comes in 10 minutes early so the issue can be dealt with.

Check-In with Educational Assistants (brief, weekly)

Educational Assistants (EAs) are the right hand for many of our classroom teachers. They most often take staggered lunches and are not available all at one time. Ask your teachers if they could plan an activity on Thursday mornings 15 minutes before the morning recess. This block during the day is the one least likely to have disruptions. Meet with the EA's for 10 uninterrupted minutes to check in with them. They rarely get a chance to voice their successes or issues that may be easily resolved if you are aware they are brewing. This ten-minute check-in, once a week, will pay off in spades. They know they are valued. And they will know that you are there to clear their path to the best of your ability, so they have productive days supporting the students in their care.

STEP 3: Building Relationships to Secure Your Foundation

Recess Room

There will always be some students in your building who need support and help with self-regulation. At every grade level, students may struggle due to a diagnosed condition, trauma in their young lives, or lack of self-esteem. Having an alternative place for these students to go during unstructured time, such as recess, benefits everyone in your building.

I would suggest that supervising the recess room be part of your duty schedule and that all staff take their turn there. This place is not for student punishment. This is an alternative to going outside. The room should be well stocked with board games for every age level. Board games and cards teach the skills of taking turns, winning, and losing, and cooperating, without the stress of physical games where the adrenaline can get pumping.

During sports games and physical activities, the students who lack self-control skills often find that they are not in the driver's seat when it comes to controlling their emotions. It is much easier to learn self-control skills during a quiet, structured situation like playing a board game, rather than out running on a playing field. The excitement of competition, physical activity, emotions of the game often limit a young person's ability to maintain self-control.

There may be a couple of Grade 8's who will offer to play a simple game with the younger students. The teacher on duty is expected to participate with students as well to role model the desired behaviors.

End of Month Assemblies

To help build a sense of community within your school, I believe that all students need to be brought together to celebrate.

Once a month, create an opportunity for students to come together for an assembly. Provide each class with an opportunity to prepare a presentation for the rest of the school. Character attributes are explained explicitly for the child's benefit. I prefer to hold these assemblies in the morning. You will know what would work best for your staff and students. Remember, this is an important learning experience for students.

These assemblies provide a venue for students to learn audience manners and appropriate behaviour.

It is important for every student to see themselves as:

- an equal peer to all other students;
- as representatives and a reflection of the school they are attending; and together,
- they are an important part of the school team.

I have included which class is responsible for which assembly in the staff handbook. They must be well organized, and good audience manners are required. The little ones can only sit still for 20 minutes so be sure to stay within that time-frame. Every class should benefit from this 20-minute experience.

Switch Around Days

Switch Around Days are a strategy to build a community atmosphere between all staff and all students.

There are many occasions in a school building when students are supervised by other staff who are not their classroom teachers. It's important that all staff in the building recognize that we are responsible for ALL students who attend our schools, not just the ones we do report cards for. I used a strategy to reinforce this mindset called "Switch Around Day". I planned three of these per year and they were included on the initial school calendar. I found it effective to have Switch Around Days in mid-October, February, and again the third week of June (Play Day). These are times during a school year where staff and students may be feeling sluggish for some reason (weather, shorter days, the excitement of beginning a new year wearing off, etc.).

Switch Around Days should have a theme. Organize the entire school into cross-grade grouping (like a play day). Match the youngest students with a buddy in Grade 7 or 8. Ask each classroom teacher to be responsible for one 30-minute activity. One activity example is Character ideas: one class makes a chain of helping hands. Each student traces their hand with the help of a friend sitting close by, cuts them out, and helps their young buddy to cut theirs out. Together, they write five ways they could demonstrate helping hands at your wonderful school. The kids' ideas are **awesome**! Another teacher may have each student draw and colour what they like to do on weekends on a "puzzle" piece. The pieces can then be put together to make a huge mural in the hallway. There are tons of Character books out there as well as ideas to be found online for each teacher to find simple 30-minute activities.

These switch around day activities are merely the means to get everyone in the school working together on joint projects. The intention of these activities are to build relationships between students and all teaching staff. It also provides a chance for each student to visit each other's classrooms in the school. It gives the students a sense of belonging when they can see what is happening behind all the doors. They are curious to see what is up on the bulletin boards, how other classrooms feel, and having the opportunity to get to know the other teachers.

This is also a time for the older students to develop their empathy skills as they get to know a younger buddy. I would encourage these buddies to do a 20-minute activity together once a week for the rest of the year. (Reading buddies only takes 10 minutes, and then they can help their younger buddy get dressed for recess. What a gift to the educators in the classroom!)

When an older student is having a hormonal day and needs a break from classmates, he or she can easily slip into their buddy's room to help for 10 minutes. Many times, we can help a student avoid having a miserable day by offering them a break and giving them a simple job to do that they can feel proud of. At some point or another all of you will have had students that would benefit from this easy strategy.

Each teacher is responsible for one activity, and they run the same activity with six groups.

School schedules are so varied. I would suggest you schedule this for the last two blocks of the day. Do 30-minute activities and then a nutrition break. Following the nutrition break, teams reassemble in the gym, and everyone wears their name tags. Put coloured dots on the different teams, so you know exactly who belongs where if someone comes back from the dentist, arrives late, or is being picked up for an appointment. You know where to look because you and every teacher and EA have a copy of the teams and the rotation schedule.

The second switch around day is usually math games and activities, and the third one is cooperative games during June's Play Day. The activities are fun and engaging for all students.

My experience at the conclusion of each Switch Around Activity Day is that everyone feels more connected. Teachers have learned a lot more names, students from other classrooms say hello to all the teachers in the hallways, out at bus time, and on yard duty.

Student-Led Conferences

Two times a year, already on your calendar.

Student-led conferences are an opportunity for each student to show their parents a folder full of work from different subject areas. These folders are usually divided into three sections: the work they are most proud of; their growth in writing and math; and, things they are working on. They take place during the school day, during the week Report Cards are sent in February, and the last week of June.

For two days, set up the gym with stations that have three to four chairs and a little table or desk. This provides a surface for the child to spread their stuff out or set up a laptop. Serve tea, coffee, and snacks to parents and guardians. Offer juice boxes with a snack for the students who are presenting their evidence of learning.

On the two days that the gym is occupied for conferences, each classroom teacher knows exactly what to do when a parent (or guardian or senior mentor) arrives. Their student simply takes their folder with them and escorts their parents to the gym along with the ambassador who is going to get them refreshments. Each student has practiced going through their folders and explaining their learning. This only takes 10 to 15 minutes.

Have each classroom teacher set up a designated Writing Bulletin Board and a Math Activity Bulletin Board in their classrooms from September until June. There is a space for each student on that board. Every month, every student adds a published piece of writing and completed math activity to the board. You can literally staple them on top of each other. If your school is lucky enough to have chrome books or iPads for each student, these can be electronic files. If not, it is worth printing and displaying. Each teacher needs to have evidence of the students' growth. Having designated bulletin boards that contain additions once a month seems to work.

Each student will take the items from the bulletin board and place them in their 3-part folders to share their progress in a demonstrative and simple way to their parents. Students use their posted accomplishments to explain and share with their parents their progress.

Each student should also have a three-part folder that contains things they are proud of. Also include items they are working on and a list of their personal goals for each term. Each section of the folder is labelled.

Have two Grade 8s' serve as ambassadors to greet your guests at the front door. (I always used six students for this job. Each pair would work the doors for one learning block per day.)

Positive Phone Calls

Each classroom teacher is responsible for making one positive telephone call every month to their student's parents/caregiver. This does not take much time; it can be as little as two minutes per phone call to say:

"Just wanted you to know how beautiful John's art was today!"

"Susie was fantastic at helping out a classmate this morning!"

This proactive, positive approach builds relationships with parents and creates an environment where the parents receive positive feedback about their kids. It also creates the opportunity for the parent to discuss matters related to their child. And it helps mitigate any anxiety the parent or student may have about getting a call from their teacher.

Agendas

Every student is presented with an agenda notebook on their first day of school. This is an opportunity that enables communication between home and school on a daily basis. Students from Grade 3 and up will learn from their teachers what is to be included in the agenda. For the younger students, it is the teacher's responsibility to send a message to the family each day. (Many teachers put a small sticker on the agenda, e.g., "Marg had a great day!"

Grade 8 Students (Getting Them to Help)

By Grade 8, students are into their adolescence and puberty. Some are maturing physically and emotionally more quickly or slowly than their friends. Some have outgrown relationships from previous years. Going through adolescence is plainly a difficult time for most students, with their bodies undergoing the physical and psychological changes of puberty. Some students feel that life is out of whack. Giving them a little extra support in their final year before high school can go long way in supporting these children emotionally.

Observe the Grade 8 kids on the playground during the first week of school. By the third recess break, you will know which may benefit from being asked to help:

- with changing the bulletin boards in Grade 3
- the kindergarten teacher getting kids dressed and undressed for the playground

- by playing with the little one in SK that has trouble keeping her hands to herself
- by being referee the Grade 2 soccer game at recess
- the librarian to help sort stuff in the library

Give these Grade 8 students a job at least one recess a week. It helps minimize the loneliness or isolation they may feel on the playground.

STEP 4: Cementing Positive Relationships in Your Building

The first four months of school are very demanding. You will need to allow yourself three hours on a Saturday or Sunday to keep up with your paperwork. Once students and staff are in your building, you need to expect a day of constant interruptions. They need an attentive Principal in the office. Remember, this is why you stepped into this challenging and rewarding position. Your time will be not your own during school hours. You will need all your wits about you to enable your staff to grow into their full potential. Your energy will be consumed remaining positive and encouraging every second you are with colleagues, students, or parents.

Communication, Communication, Communication

Distribute all documents: Handbooks; Calendars; Newsletters; and, Monday Memos, electronically and as hard copies (even if you know that every one of your students has high speed internet). While it may be 2022, many of our students' primary caregivers may not have access to computers, as we learned during the pandemic. The form of communication is not what is important here. Making sure ALL our caregivers get the school information is.

Thank You Cards

Make a trip to the dollar store and stock up on a hundred Thank You cards. Make list of the names of every member of your staff and the months across the top. This will help you to easily keep track who you have sent cards to and who may need one. Some of the obvious ones are teachers who take on extra-curricular activities, helping a colleague with yard duty, or helping a student tie their shoes. Anything you observe as caring and thoughtful provides an opportunity for a thank you. E.g., "When you thought I wasn't looking, I saw you taking a few extra minutes with Johnny, whose dog died." It takes a minute or less to thank them for the time they are giving to our students. Pop it in their mailbox. These simple gestures uplift your staff. It encourages them to be more productive in their classrooms.

Also pass the bus driver a card and thank him or her for being kind to the students on their bus. The kids will see you passing the card. They do not miss a trick. Walk to the crosswalk and pass the crossing guard a thank you. If you have any volunteers in your building for breakfast program or reading time – anything at all – be sure to thank them, each month, as well. The little time this takes will reap great benefits. These cards can be part of your three-hour work block on the weekend when no one else is in the building to interrupt you.

*See also the previous **Building Positive Relationships** section of this manual for additional information on cards.*

Find the Great Thing

No one survives the demands of a classroom teacher if they do not possess several talents. Some of our staff shine like stars. Others may need some polishing. Every teacher has some qualities that help them relate to their students. For some it may be difficult to find their spark. These are the teachers you need to watch closely as they start their year. As soon as you see something positive, you need to jump on it like a panther and compliment that staff member (in front of colleagues) for their accomplishment. But remember, **appreciation and compliments must be authentic**. This intentional drawing out of the teacher's talents will boost their confidence, which you want them to demonstrate to students.

Note: If you are stuck and cannot find one thing to genuinely compliment, call the previous Principal and discuss that person's good qualities. Everyone has them. Some are people whose gifts are hard to find. They are in there somewhere. Otherwise, they would not have pursued teaching. In three months, you will see your staff walking with their heads held high.

Sincere expressions of appreciation develop strong relationships!

Staff Socials

VERY IMPORTANT: Schedule three get-togethers with your staff each year and invite their spouses/ partners and children.

My husband and I had a small, modest home, but we held these get-togethers at our place. These were very casual, with some dollar store activities for kids of various ages, beverages provided for all (soft drinks, beer and wine) and pizza with vegetable trays and a large garden salad. That's it. It will likely cost you $200, and it's a fantastic return on investment. People appreciate being invited. It only needs to be a couple of hours, from 5:00 to 7:00 p.m.

If this idea does not work for you, perhaps there is a local restaurant where you can meet for happy hour with your staff. You can pay for shared appetizers. There are various options available for these social events. It is simply a gesture that you, as their leader, recognize how hard they are working. APPRECIATION is so important in a school setting and most often is in short supply.

Schedule the first get-together on the first Thursday evening of the school year to welcome everyone back. Have the second one at the end of February when staff are tired and need a lift. The third one should be held near the end of June.

In a school setting, we know exactly when the stressful times occur and when everyone needs a boost. Report card time, Christmas, November, and February are low months for morale. In June, your teachers are very stressed, wondering if they did enough for each student before they move into their next class. There is not a teacher on earth who does not struggle with end-of-year report cards. Make sure you let each teacher know that you appreciate how hard it is. If you have a staff of 30 or less, you can write every person a thank you card for the time they are putting in. Leave a treat on everyone's desk or show up with coffee for everyone. The sky is the limit. If staff know you appreciate how hard they are working and understand that it's a tough time of year, they will give you 150%.

Two Over Ten (A Strategy for Classroom Teachers)

This strategy is included in the Staff Handbook. The Elementary Teachers Federation of Ontario (EFTO) suggests a "two over ten" strategy for classroom teachers. This is how it works: take two minutes for 10 consecutive school days and talk to a student who is having trouble settling into the classroom routines. This conversation can happen in the hallway, yard duty, when they are eating their lunch, arriving in the morning, or as they are catching their bus home. Two minutes a day sounds easy, but it isn't. Although difficult, it is very beneficial. ETFO suggests targeting only one student at a time because it is easier to manage that with intentional effort for the ten days. You will begin to see a difference after the sixth or seventh day, but don't stop there. Make sure you do 10 consecutive days. The results are incredible. That student will feel that you have time for them as an individual and you want to get to know them a little better. This also benefits the teacher. We want every teacher's energy conserved for positive interactions and growth. We do not want them spending any of their precious energy on feeling stressed about interacting with some students. IT WORKS! You can check in with the teacher every few days to ask how this experiment is going.

Wrap Up

The formula for success requires some up-front time and effort. Most of the work involved can be done ahead of time. The benefits will far outweigh the time needed to set things up. You should put all these elements in place as soon as you know your placement for the following year. If you are an administrator at a school over many years, you will just have to tweak these templates. Follow this formula and you will LOVE to go to work every day, with motivated, happy staff!

This approach to managing your building will give your thriving school the foundation to soar!!!

My wish is that you find this information helpful in defining your own leadership style, philosophy and principles.

May you help children grow and blossom into their full potential.

Thank you!

I want to thank **Miss Scott**, my Grade Five teacher at Alex Muir School in Sault Ste. Marie. In 1967, Miss Scott showed me the importance of being kind to every student in the classroom each and every day.

Thank you to **Eva MacKenna**, for changing the trajectory of my career in one simple sentence.

Thank you to **Christa Wright** who always made sure every child, staff and parent was treated with kindness, dignity, and gentleness no matter what the circumstance or problem.

Thank you to my editors **Patrick Leroux, Kellie Garrett, Jan and Cliff Prowse and my husband, Tom**.

Thank you to **Frank Palumbo** for having a full year calendar hanging in his school foyer.

Thank you to **Lu Reece** for demonstrating how a recess room worked.

Thank you to **Shelly Gold** for reinforcing how much fun our job is, to find humour in things, and to laugh with your staff.

Thank you to **Joanne McKenzie** for demonstrating how important it is to show your staff that you know they have the hardest job in the building.

Thank you to **Pam Cooper** for teaching me never to forget to thank all the helpers that work to keep our school building ship shape.

Thank you to my sister **Barb** who suggested I write down my recipe for building relationships in the school community.

Thank you to **Erin Lodge**, CEO of SocialEManagement for designing my webpage, marketing, communications, and promotion. I especially want to thank her for all her time, energy, patience, and unwavering encouragement to get this project off the ground!

Finally, I want to thank all the wonderful staff that I had the amazing opportunity to work with. Staff that saw that Mother's Day and Father's Day were taking too much of a toll on students who were struggling with their family situation, and suggested we change and celebrate Family Day instead. The staff that made sure kids got to hockey practices, and who sat and cried with them when their dogs died. The staff that made a point of walking with a child who was by themselves outside on recess. You have all set the ripples in motion. Our world is a kinder, more compassionate place because you planted the seeds of compassion and kindness in all your students.

Attachments

This last section of the manual contains; a sample copy of the Calendars; Staff Handbook; Family Handbook; along with samples of a Monday Memo, Signage and Monthly Newsletter. All this information is available for download at www.margdodds.com. There are templates to modify for your own use.

They are there to save you time and money and can avoid "re-inventing the wheel". Use what is useful and fits with your school philosophy. You can simply add your school logo and fill in the spaces for your school and staff or tweak it however you like. I hope you find them helpful.

The calendar enclosed and on the website includes a First Nation Grandfather Teachings/ Character Attribute for each month. Of course, these attributes overlap all year long. We want students to understand these virtues and how we incorporate them into our lives every day.

I wish you much joy in doing the work you do every day to make the world a better place. You are setting ripples in motion. All the best on your fabulous adventure in leading the leaders of tomorrow.

School Calendar

Sample Template

September 2022

Grandfather Teaching: Perseverance

Perseverance/Resiliency

During this month the students are going to be learning about striving to do their best, motivating themselves to keep trying and never giving up on something they want to do. Each class will discuss becoming strong, healthy and successful following difficulties. Orange Shirt Day to celebrate Residential School Survivors will be on September 30th.

Sunday	Monday	Tuesday	Wednesday	Thursday	Friday	Saturday
				1 Professional Development Day	2	3
4	5 Labour Day	6 Welcome Back! First Day for our Wonderful Students and Staff!!!	7	8	9 Welcome Back Assembly (Daily schedules due in the office)	10
11	12 (Supply teacher folders due in the office)	13 Tuesday Folder	14 Staff Meeting 3:40	15 Primary In-School Meeting	16	17
18	19	20 Tuesday Folder	21 Healthy School Committee Meeting 10:40	22 Junior In-School Meeting	23 Professional Development Day	24
25	26 Parent Council 6:00	27 Tuesday Folder	28	29 Intermediate In-School Meeting	30 Orange Shirt Day End of Month Assembly	

Parents and guardians, we are SO HAPPY to have your children with us each and every day! Please let the school know if your daughter/son has any concerns. We look forward to seeing them every day. If they are going to be absent, please call the school and let us know.

OCTOBER 2022

Grandfather Teaching: Humility

Humility

Humility is to know that you are very special and a gift to our community. Respect yourself and carry your pride by being gentle, calm and patient with others. You understand that you are equal to others and not better. You live your life with compassion.

Sunday	Monday	Tuesday	Wednesday	Thursday	Friday	Saturday
2	3	4	5	6 Primary In-School Meeting	7 (Long range plans due in office)	8
9	Thanksgiving	11 Tuesday Folder	12	13 Junior In-School Meeting	14 Switch Around Day 11:30-3:30	15
16	17	18 Tuesday Folder	19 Healthy School Committee Meeting 10:40	20 Intermediate In-School Meeting	21 Professional Development Day	22
23	24	25 Tuesday Folder	26 Staff Meeting 3:40	27 Halloween Family Dance 5:00-7:00 Scholastic Book Fair	28 Scholastic Book Fair	29
30 Parent Council 6:00	31 End of Month School Assembly Halloween					

PARENTS/GUARDIANS – Please join us for our HALLOWEEN FAMILY DANCE, October 27th from 5:00-7:00! With the weather getting cooler, please remember that your children love their recesses, so they need to be dressed for the cooler weather. Time to get out the winter boots, hats and mittens. Winter here we come!

NOVEMBER 2022

Grandfather Teaching: Respect

Respect

Value others for the goodness they share.

Accept that each individual person experiences and understands life differently.

Remember each of us is special. We should never ask anyone or force anyone to be different for us.

Sunday	Monday	Tuesday	Wednesday	Thursday	Friday	Saturday
		1	2	3	4	5
6	7 PARENT MEETING 6PM	8 Tuesday Folder	9 Healthy School Committee Meeting 10:40	10 Primary In-School Meeting	11 REMEMBRACE DAY CEREMONY 10:45 AM	12
13	14 Canned Food Drive begins	15 PROGRESS REPORTS IN Tuesday Folder	16 Family Math Night 5:00-6:30	17 Junior In-School Meeting	18 LAST DAY FOR Canned Food DriVE	19
20	21	22 Tuesday Folder	23 Principal's Meeting	24 Intermediate In-School Meeting	25	26
27	28	29 Tuesday Folder	30 END OF MONTH ASSEMBLY 10AM			

The shorter days and cooler weather is upon us. Please make sure your little ones are appropriately dressed for the colder, rainy weather. We invite everyone to join us for our Remembrance Day Assembly, November 11 th . We ask you to be seated by 10:45 so we have our moment of silence with the rest of our grateful nation promptly at 11:00a.m. Also we invite you to Family math night to play a variety of games involving math with your children, enjoy refreshments, and FUN!!!

DECEMBER 2022

Grandfather Teaching: Love

Love

Share Kindness. Living a good life helps us to take care of others and to be cared for by others. It is normal to disagree with people we love and care for. Love is to know peace. Love is unconditional. Mutual love flows back and forth. Weak people need more love. It is of most importance to love and care for yourself.

Sunday	Monday	Tuesday	Wednesday	Thursday	Friday	Saturday
		Tuesday Folder		1 Primary In-School Meeting	2	3
4	5 PARENT MEETING 6:00	6 Tuesday Folder	7	8 Junior In-School Meeting	9	10
11	12	13 Tuesday Folder	14 Healthy School Meeting 10:40 AM	15 Intermediate In-School Meeting	16	17
18	19	20 DRESS REHEARSAL FOR HOLIDAY CONCERT 10:45 - 12 NOON	21 HOLIDAY CONCERT 6PM	22	23 End of Month ASSEMBLY	24 Christmas Eve
25 Christmas Day	26	27	28	29	30	31

WHAT A GREAT FOUR months we have had with your children!
We wish each of you a happy holiday season and look forward to a fabulous 2023 with you!!!
Also, just a reminder to have your child take all their belongings home over the break,
so our care staff can give the school a thorough cleaning to start the New Year with a clean and shiny school!!!!

JANUARY 2023

Grandfather Teaching: Honesty & Integrity

Honesty & Integrity

Always be honest in your words and actions. If you are honest with yourself, it is easier to be honest with others. Always do the right thing. Tell the whole truth. Never cheat or steal. Be your BEST self everyday!

Sunday	Monday	Tuesday	Wednesday	Thursday	Friday	Saturday
1	2	3 TUESDAY FOLDER	4	5 PRIMARY IN-SCHOOL MEETING	6	7
8	9	10 TUESDAY FOLDER	11	12 JUNIOR IN-SCHOOL MEETING	13	14
15	16	17 TUESDAY FOLDER	18 HEALTHY SCHOOL COMMITTEE MEETING 10:40	19 STAFF MEETING 3:40	20	21
22	23	24 TUESDAY FOLDER	25	26 INTERMEDIATE IN-SCHOOL MEETING	27	28
29	30 END OF MONTH ASSEMBLY PARENT COUNCIL 6:00					

Welcome Back!!!

What a fabulous 2022 we are going to have! Your teachers have been busy planning fantastic learning experiences for you! Parents, please remember that January weather is unpredictable. When the temperature dips to -20 the students will be inside for all breaks. Thank you for sending your child to school with appropriate winter clothing.

FEBRUARY 2023

Grandfather Teaching: Truth

Truth

Speak from the heart. Always speak the truth to yourself and others. To tell someone exactly what we mean is to be truthful. These teaching were given for people to share with each other to have a good life.

Sunday	Monday	Tuesday	Wednesday	Thursday	Friday	Saturday
	30	31 TUESDAY FOLDER	1	2 PRIMARY IN-SCHOOL MEETING	3 PROFESSIONAL DEVELOPMENT DAY	4
5	6 STUDENT-LED CONFERENCES 9:00-2:30	7 STUDENT-LED CONFERENCES TUESDAY FOLDER	8 STAFF MEETING 3:40	9 JUNIOR IN-SCHOOL MEETING	10	11
12	13	14 HAPPY VALENTINE'S DAY Red & white day TUESDAY FOLDER	15 HEALTHY SCHOOL COMMITTEE MEETING 10:40	16 INTERMEDIATE IN-SCHOOL	17	18
19	20 FAMILY DAY (NO SCHOOL)	21 TUESDAY FOLDER	22 PINK SHIRT DAY	23 FAMILY DANCE 5 - 7PM	24	25
26	27 END OF MONTH ASSEMBLY	28				

We are looking forward to seeing you during out two days of Student-led Conferences. Anytime between 9:30-2:30 on Monday or Tuesday, February 6 and 7th, you are welcome to come to your son/daughter's classroom. They will get their portfolio of work to share with you and escort you to the gym where you will be served a beverage while your child shows you their accomplishments for this term!

Also, we are having a family dance to celebrate Family Day on Thursday, February 24th! Hope to see you there!

March 2023

Bravery

Always do what you know is right. Do the right thing even when it is scary and the consequences might be unpleasant. Stand up for the right of others. You have a strong, fearless heart! To have the mental and moral strength to overcome fears that prevent us from helping others and living our best life. Share courage, not aggression. You being kind and loving helps you to live a good life.

Sunday	Monday	Tuesday	Wednesday	Thursday	Friday	Saturday
		1 TUESDAY FOLDER	2	3 PRIMARY IN-SCHOOL MEETING	4	5
6	7	8 TUESDAY FOLDER	9 STAFF MEETING 3:40	9 JUNIOR IN-SCHOOL MEETING	10	11
12	13	14	15	16	17	18
		M A R C H B R E A K				
19	20 PARENT COUNCIL	21 TUESDAY FOLDER	22 HEALTHY SCHOOL COMMITTEE MEETING 10:40	23 INTERMEDIATE IN-SCHOOL MEETING	24	25
26	27	28 TUESDAY FOLDER	29	30 END OF MONTH ASSEMBLY		

It has been a busy term for all our students and staff. We wish you a restful and happy March Break. Please consider joining us at our Parent Council meeting on March 21 st for coffee and chat. Always welcome concerns or questions. Also a reminder all parent s are welcome at our end of month assemblies!

APRIL 2023

Grandfather Teaching: Responsibility

Responsibility

All students are responsible for what they do and say. Our students are learning to be reliable and dependable. Always do what you say you are going to do. Accept the consequences of all your actions.

Sunday	Monday	Tuesday	Wednesday	Thursday	Friday	Saturday
	4	5 TUESDAY FOLDER	6	7 PRIMARY IN-SCHOOL MEETING	8	9
10	11 PARENT MEETING 6PM	12 TUESDAY FOLDER	13 HEALTHY SCHOOL COMMITTEE MEETING 10:40	14 JUNIOR IN-SCHOOL MEETING	15	16
17 EASTER	18 EASTER MONDAY	19 TUESDAY FOLDER	20	21 INTERMEDIATE IN-SCHOOL MEETING	22 PROFESSIONAL DEVELOPMENT DAY	23
24	25	26 TUESDAY FOLDER	27 STAFF MEETING 3:40	28	29 END OF MONTH SCHOOL ASSEMBLY 10 AM	30

Parents and guardians, we are SO HAPPY to have your children with us each and every day! Please let the school know if your daughter/son has any concerns. We look forward to seeing them every day. If they are going to be absent, please call the school and let us know.

MAY 2023

Grandfather Teaching: Cooperation/Collaboration

Cooperation/Collaboration

Our school we encourage all students to work together. Our students and staff help each other out. We share our talents and gifts with each other and help each other out at every opportunity. We encourage our students to ask adults for help when they need it.

Sunday	Monday	Tuesday	Wednesday	Thursday	Friday	Saturday
1	2 READ A BOOK TO YOUR PARENTS DAY! EDUCATION WEEK	3 TUESDAY FOLDER	4 MATH GALLERY ON DSIPLAY IN THE GYM PARENTS WELCOME 9:30 - 2:30PM	5	6	7
8	BEGINS 9	10 TUESDAY FOLDER	11 HEALTHY SCHOOL COMMITTEE MEETING 10:40	12 PRIMARY IN-SCHOOL MEETING	13	14
15	16	17 TUESDAY FOLDER	18	19 JUNIOR IN-SCHOOL MEETING	20 PROFESSIONAL DEVELOPMENT DAY	21
22	23 VICTORIA DAY	24 TUESDAY FOLDER	2 5 STAFF MEETING 3:40	26 INTERMEDIATE IN-SCHOOL MEETING	27	28
29	30 PARENT COUNCIL 6:00	TUESDAY 31 FOLDER END OF MONTH ASSEMBLY				

The days are getting longer and we know it is harder to get the kids to bed when the birds are singing and the sun is shining. We still have 2 months of great learning time. All our teachers are keeping their classroom routines to try to minimize "Spring Fever" in the building. Parents of Grade 3 and 6 students, please try not to schedule any doctor or dentist appointments during the EQAO testing days the last week of May and first week of June. Your help is very much appreciated.

JUNE 2023

Grandfather Teaching: Wisdom

Wisdom

You gain wisdom by practicing Love, Respect, Bravery, Honesty, Humility and Truth. The building of a healthy community is dependent on each member to use the gifts of their own spirit to contribute to the development of a peaceful and healthy Community. This is Wisdom.

Sunday	Monday	Tuesday	Wednesday	Thursday	Friday	Saturday
				1	2	3
4	5 PARENT COUNCIL 6:00 (Review Calendar for next year)	6 TUESDAY FOLDER	7 HEALTHY SCHOOL COMMITTEE MEETING 10:40	8	9 PROFESSIONAL DEVELOPMENT DAY	10
11	12	13 TUESDAY FOLDER	14 Staff Meeting 3:40 (We will be reviewing next year's calendar)	15	16	17
18	19	20 TUESDAY FOLDER	21	22	23 SWITCH AROUND PLAY DAY	24
25	26 STUDENT-LED CONFERENCES (9:30-2:30)	27 STUDENT-LED CONFERENCES LAST TUESDAY FOLDER	28	29 END OF MONTH ASSEMBLY 9:15		

Looking forward to seeing you on the 27thor 28th.Please help us to get the school ready for a thorough summer clean by making sure your child's belongings are collected and taken home by the 29th. Any unclaimed shoes, jackets, and clothing will be washed and donated to the soup kitchen on June 30th.

Staff Handbook

STAFF
HANDBOOK

 PURPOSE OF INFORMATION BOOKLET

The main purpose of spending time at school is to gain the academic knowledge and skills that will help you to succeed in the future. In order to accomplish this goal, we must work co-operatively as members of a team. We need to have rules and ways of doing things that everyone understands so that we know what is expected of each of us as we go about our daily work.

WELCOME

Welcome to the 2021-2022 school year at ? School! It is a pleasure to begin the school year with such a dedicated group of teachers.

Hopefully, the information in this handbook will help you with school routines and procedures, as well as with program planning and assessment.

Please do not hesitate to ask questions or make suggestions. We are strongest when we work together. Here's to a great year ahead!

AND WE'RE OFF!

WITHIN THIS HANDBOOK YOU WILL FIND:

staff handbook

→ CONTENTS

→ AND WE ARE OFF!

DAILY SCHEDULE
- 8:50 -10:30 am Instructional Time
- 10:30-11:15 am Nutrition Break
- 11:15-12:55 pm Instructional Time
- 12:55- 1:40 pm Nutrition Break/Recess
- 1:40- 3:20 pm Instructional Time

ENTRY AND EXIT PROCEDURES

It is expected that students will enter and exit the building as politely, quickly, and safely as possible. When breaks are over, teachers are asked to move to their doorways or hallways quickly and remain there until their students are in class. Students should know exactly what to do upon entering the room. Waiting for the teacher to tell them what to do often leads to off-task behaviour. After entering at each break there should be a set routine to get them engaged and settled immediately upon entry.

STUDENT DISMISSAL

Students must be ready for dismissal no earlier than 3:15. Our buses arrive promptly at 3:20. Students are to head down to the buses as close to 3:20 as possible.

There is no supervision for students who arrive early for the buses, so please supervise students in your classroom and in the hallway prior to them leaving for the buses or exiting the building.

No student is to leave the building prior to the bell unless he/she has parental permission – students should have a note in their agendas to verify their parent's permission.

Thank you for ensuring that students vacate the hallways in a prompt and orderly fashion. If a student misses the bus, the teacher on duty and principal will make sure that the student gets home safely.

→ AND WE ARE OFF!

YARD SUPERVISION
Please post the supervision schedule in your classroom.

EXPECTED YARD BEHAVIOUR
- Safety First
- Practice hands-off and feet-off at all times
- Show respect and demonstrate qualities of good character
- Play fairly and inclusively (e.g. You can't say, "you can't play")
- Use appropriate language and gentle words (name-calling, teasing and put downs will never be tolerated)
- Things on the ground, stay on the ground (sticks, stones, snowballs)

YARD SUPERVISION GUIDELINES
- Be on time.
- Move around as much as possible.
- Be alert for problems. Early intervention is our best defence.
- Send in another child if there is an emergency and you require additional assistance. Avoid bringing children to the office when you are on duty.
- Have offenders walk with you while on duty if they have done something minor. Bring problems to my attention upon entering the building, if necessary.
- All injuries must be reported to the office. Forms must be completed for serious injuries. Keep the classroom teacher informed and notify the home for most injuries. All head injuries (even if you consider them minor) must be reported to the office and the classroom teacher. In addition, a call must be made home. The first aid kit is located in the office under the fax machine. Record all first aid treatment. Please note the eye wash station location.
- During indoor recess, walk around the school, checking on each room. Please ensure students have suitable activities during indoor recess. (If you need more board games, let me know). We will continue the games room.
- There should be no students left in a classroom or in other areas of the school unsupervised at any time.

→ AND WE ARE OFF!

CHARACTER EDUCATION

Character Education is a big part of what we do in our classrooms, in the hallway and on the yard. We specifically address character attributes monthly at our assemblies. It comes down to two questions when we are assessing appropriate/inappropriate behaviour:

- Was it kind?
- Was it respectful?

MESSAGES AND ASSEMBLIES

Character Assemblies are held monthly. The purpose of the assembly is to provide an opportunity for the school community to come together to celebrate student success and learn more about the Character Attribute for the next month. Although not required, classes/choirs or clubs are welcome to make presentations at the assemblies. Please let me know at least a week ahead of time if this is the case so we can ensure that our assemblies are kept to 20 minutes.

The classes responsible for the character assemblies each month are as follows:

Month	Attribute	Class
September	Resiliency/Perseverance	Principal
October	Humility	Grade 6/7
November	Respect	Grade 7/8
December	Love	Grade 4
January	Honesty/Integrity	Grade 1/2
February	Truth	Grade 5
March	Bravery	Grade 2/3
April	Responsibility	Grade 3/4
May	Cooperation/Collaboration	Grade SK/1
June	Wisdom	Grade 7/8

→ AND WE ARE OFF!

RAINY DAYS/INCLEMENT WEATHER PROCEDURES

When buses arrive in the morning on wet or extremely cold days, the children are to enter and go to the breakfast room or their classrooms. Teachers on duty are to patrol the halls (one in the primary wing, the other in the junior/intermediate wing). It is the decision of the teacher on duty as to whether or not the children go outside or come in early during recesses on wet or very cold days. The bell and announcement indicate an indoor recess. Teachers on duty patrol the halls during these times. Any additional teacher supervision in the classrooms is always welcome.

LUNCH TIME ROUTINES

Students will remain in their own classrooms' during the lunch period. Please post and review guidelines for acceptable and expected lunchtime behaviour. September is an important month to establish and set old routines. (I would very much appreciate all teachers remaining in their classrooms for the first 10 minutes of lunch for the first week of school to establish routines. If this is done in the beginning, we should reap the benefits throughout the school year).

DAILY PLANS/DAYBOOK

Your daily plans should be kept on your desktop. Clearly indicate children with severe allergies, custody problems, etc. Please keep a supply teacher folder readily available. Run off some extra activities in case the supply teacher needs to fill some time. Your daily schedule should include the components of a comprehensive literacy program and a 75-minute math block. I will continue to keep your two-day emergency folders in the office.

LONG-RANGE PLANS

Please hand in your daily schedule, including preparation periods, by September 9th, 2022. Long-range plans are due at the office by October 7th, 2022. Also, please hand in Supply Teacher Folders with schedule by September 12th, 2022. (This folder will only be used in case of emergencies)

→ AND WE ARE OFF!

SAFE ARRIVAL POLICY/STUDENT ABSENCES

Please ensure that attendance is entered into your compputer at 9:00 am and 1:45 pm. If you know why a student is absent, please write the reason for absence in the space provided. Also, if a student arrives after the attendance has been sent down to the office, please notify the office of the student's arrival if they have not already checked in at the office. These steps will save us a call in the office and avoid undue worry for our parents.

If students are leaving the school during the day (medical appointments, etc.) attach the note to the attendance form. As students return to the classroom or arrive late, make sure they have stopped at the office. Students taking music lessons are not marked absent.

Students who have been suspended are not marked absent: mark a "G" in the space.

ANNOUNCEMENTS

"O' Canada" and the announcements occur after the students are settled at 8:55. The first bell rings at 8:50. There is a binder beside the P.A. system in the office that has dated announcement sheets. Please feel free to put your announcements in the book. Grade 8 students will make the announcements as well as character messages each morning before "O' Canada."

CURRICULUM NIGHT AND FAMILY BARBEQUE

This evening is used to inform parents about the Ministry Guidelines as well as report cards. Please take the time to explain classroom routines, the homework policy, and your expectations as classroom teacher. Parents will support you if they are aware of what you expect from their child. Curriculum Night and Welcome Back Barbeque will be September 14th, 2022, 5:00 to 7:00 pm (BARBEQUE 5:00-6:00). Meet in the gym at 6:00, classroom visits at 6:15, 6:30 and 6:45.

CHILDREN'S AID SOCIETY (CAS)

Please remember it is your responsibility to report any suspected child abuse (physical, sexual, or emotional). If you have any questions or concerns, I am available to assist. (CAS -949-0162) ask for a child protection worker). The form you must complete after making the call is at the Secretary's office. If possible, I would appreciate knowing you have called.

→ AND WE ARE OFF!

HOME COMMUNICATION

Please keep me informed about your classroom's special activities, programs and routines. I need to see all home communication before sending it home. If you anticipate an upset parent, I would appreciate knowing this. It is easier for me to support your decision and/or plans if I have accurate background information.

NEWSLETTERS

I welcome any articles or items for our school newsletters. (Please hand in to me the 3rd week of the month, as we prepare it to go home the Tuesday before a new month). We will continue to send it home at the end of the month, with a calendar for the following month with any additions or deletions to our original calendar.

OSR FILES

Student OSR files are kept in the office. As report cards are prepared, a copy should be placed in the student's files. OSR files are not to leave the school and must be returned to the office before the end of each day. The information in the OSR is available to the school's supervisory officers, principals and teachers only for the purpose of improving the instruction of the student. Parents have the right to examine the OSR and to receive a copy of its contents. The following material is filed in the OSR folder – Report Cards, Response Forms, Formal Suspension Notices, Cards recording the students' accumulated instruction in FSL, and any addition information considered relevant for improving the instruction of the student. Documentation file, if required, might include materials such as verification of a custody, or a change of name order, psychological, health or educational assessment reports, or information on placement decisions.

SECRETARY'S OFFICE/TELEPHONE USE

The secretary's work hours are from 8:30 to 4:00 pm. One of her tasks is to ensure that all students are accounted for. Attendance must be input at 9:00 in the morning and 1:45 afternoon . We are mandated to follow a Safe Arrive Policy, which involves contacting the home if the school has not been notified about absences. Parents are encouraged to leave messages before 8:30 am on the phone about late arrivals, early pick ups or absences.

→ AND WE ARE OFF!

CARE STAFF

Custodians name will be here during the day from 7:30am to 4:30. Please encourage our students to pick up after themselves, especially in the hallways where there is lots of traffic. Each of you should assign monthly monitors for this.

Shoes must be off the floor for better cleaning. Monitor this please. Consider assigning a student monitor. Please clean the shelves of books and food containers weekly. Have your students clean up any spills or messes in your classrooms. We are teaching responsibility.

TELEPHONE PYRAMID

An updated pyramid is included in this package. Make sure you check the accuracy of your telephone number. Please post your pyramid at home by your phone.

STAFF ABSENCE

If you are going to be absent, please call me at home before 11:00 pm or from 7:00-7:15 am. I will then call the Board to arrange for a supply teacher. You must call the school by 2:30 pm to let us know that you will be returning the following day. The board provides supply teacher folders, where information can be kept. This folder must be kept in a visible, accessible place. Please give to me for signing by the third week of September.

Your daybook is a record of where you have been and an outline of where you are going. Its major purpose is to assist you in planning the program for your students. The daybook must be made available to supply teachers. If you take it home, arrange for is delivery to the school. Whenever possible, your daybook should be left at school.

STUDENTS OUT OF CLASSROOM

Know where your students are at all times. If someone is out of the classroom, check to see that they have gone where expected and have returned promptly. Hold regular washroom breaks or establish a procedure for one student at a time to leave the room for the washroom; whichever is most appropriate to your students and grade level. Students should not be left unsupervised in your classroom during the activity breaks.

→ AND WE ARE OFF!

EMERGENCY SCHOOL PROCEDURE

Name of location is the location for our students if an emergency causes a necessary evacuation. Classroom teachers accompany their students and remain with them until further instructions. Staff with non-teaching duties remain at the school to assist. The early bus dismissal procedure is followed in case of early dismissal due to adverse weather conditions. In the event the schools are closed during adverse weather, please let me know if it is unsafe for you to come to work.

If our workplace is not accessible due to a furnace breakdown, etc., our alternate workplace is xxx.

The Emergency Response plan has been finalized and everyone should be familiar with it.

Review the fire emergency plan.

FIRE DRILLS

There will be at least three fire drills in the fall and spring. Students must know their exit route and alternate exit route. Students should be able to vacate within 45-50 seconds. Practice from your classroom, library, gym, etc. Ensure that the last student closes the classroom door. Post fire exit signs above your classroom door, inside the classroom. Take a class list with your emergency folder with you during the fire drill. Every student must be accounted for.

LOCKDOWN/CODE RED DRILL

In case of an intruder in the school, we will announce, "CODE RED", initiate "LOCK DOWN" procedures. Please review the Code Red procedures in this binder and ensure that copies of these are posted by the exit door with your emergency folder in your classroom. Please post the "red dot" in your classroom. I will explain the red dots to the students during our Welcome Back to School Assembly. (The red dots are posted in every room and in the event that there is a lockdown, all the students sit quietly, as close to the red dot as possible. This is the most secluded area of each room.)

→ AND WE ARE OFF!

TOURS / CLASSROOM OUTINGS

Please complete the Education Tour Form at least two weeks prior to the tour (the forms are included in this book). Hopefully, we will be able to spread the tours throughout the school year so that the children and parents realize the outing is an integral part of the curriculum.

SWITCH AROUND ACTIVITY DAYS

I would like to have 3 Special Activity Days where the students are put on teams and circulate to different activities. I believe that this is a team building event for both students and staff. Students get a chance to interact with other grade levels and it provides the 7/8 class the opportunity to demonstrate their leadership skills. It also gives students in the school an opportunity to see all the other classrooms and this may develop a relationship between students that will grow as the year goes on. I would like these to occur on Friday, October 14th (Character Activities), Feb 18th (Math Day Activities), and June 24th (Play Day). Any other ideas are always welcome!

CHARACTER EDUCATION/GRANDFATHER TEACHINGS

This should be woven into your classroom in many subject areas. The focus on character education lays the foundation for academic excellence. The better students feel about themselves, the more motivated they are to do their best. The seeds of character are planted and now it is up to us as a staff to cultivate that and help it grow. We will see students take more pride in their work and want to do their best. Remember, don't judge a book by its cover or one bad apple doesn't spoil the rest. Out of a school of 220 students, the majority follow the rules, are kind and do their best. We want to focus on that and not just the minority who do not. One of the strategies that will be used this year is the Bucket Filler philosophy. Each of you has a copy to read to your class. (Yes, even Grade 8! A gentle reminder.) We will also do Random Acts of Kindness during the month of February, so in your planning, please include several specific assignments that demonstrate this. As a staff, we can put this into practice by cleaning and organizing the supply room, sports cupboard, or staff room, leaving someone a kind note, or by recognizing a colleague's strengths. There are many ways to infuse character into your lessons (especially in Language) and we have many mentor texts with excellent messages that can start very good dialogue.

→ AND WE ARE OFF!

STAFF INFORMATION

I will continue to provide you with the weekly "Monday Memo", which outlines any events, announcements etc. for the week. Please check your mailbox each Friday for this. There will also be a copy in the staff binder on the podium in the staff room. I will try for Friday noon to help with your planning for the following week. Please let me know if you have any items that you want me to include. Any flyers, postings or additional information will be placed in the staff room binder behind a copy of the "Monday Memo" for that week. Please check the staff binder daily for new information.

Please remember to record outings on the wall calendar in the hallway. I will include this information in our monthly newsletter. Thank you!

SCHEDULES

Please use the enclosed timetabling guidelines and submit a copy of your timetable/daily schedule by Friday, September 9th, 2022.

It is expected that all lessons and activities will be meaningful and based on curriculum expectations.

PROGRAM PLANNING

All program planning should begin with learning goals selected by the teacher, based on expectations from the Ontario Curriculum and reworded into student-friendly language.

Once students understand the specifics of what they are to learn, they will need to know what that learning looks like, i.e. the success criteria. Teachers (alone or with colleagues) deconstruct the curriculum expectation(s) to identify the success criteria. This ensures a solid, common understanding prior to sharing success criteria (at levels 3 and 4) with students.

In his book Visible Learning for Teachers, John Hattie encourages schools to "...consider the nature and quality of the learning intentions (goals) and success criteria and how these relate to the different levels of surface and deep understandings." (p. 166)

→ AND WE ARE OFF!

PROGRAM PLANNING CONT.,

In our Professional Learning meetings, we will discuss the importance of slowing down and really thinking about how we construct both our learning goals and success criteria to ensure that we are both effective and consistent in our use. We will work together on this by division.

This year, we will also discuss the value of including all four achievement categories of knowledge and skills when constructing our success criteria (knowledge and understanding, thinking, communication and application).

Descriptive Feed back is among the most powerful teaching and learning practices. In the Growing Success document, one of the seven fundamental principles of assessment is to provide ongoing descriptive feedback that is clear, specific, meaningful, and timely to support improved learning and achievement. Hattie refers to this as "Just in time, just for me." feedback.

In Making Classroom Assessment Work, Anne Davies refers to "specific", descriptive feedback that tells students about their learning. They find out what is working ('do more of this') and what is not ('do less of this'). They can use this information to adjust what they're doing to become more successful and to learn from their mistakes." (p.16)

For the above to occur, several things need to be put in place.

- Students must be presented with challenging tasks that are rich with feedback. Tasks that are not authentic and do not challenge students decrease motivation to learn and render feedback redundant.

- Errors provide opportunities for feedback. Therefore, a positive, caring, respectful climate is a prior condition to learning. Students must see that effort and deliberate practice will help them attain their learning goal(s). We must "start to emphasize increased effort and progress [and stop overemphasizing ability]." (Hattie, p.82)

→ AND WE ARE OFF!

PROGRAM PLANNING CONT.,

Nike has a powerful commercial featuring Michael Jordan reflecting on his success. The script goes as follows:

"I've missed more than 9000 shots in my career. I've lost almost 300 games. 26 times I've been trusted to take the game winning shot...and missed. I've failed over and over and over again in my life. And that is why I succeed."

- We must become evaluators of our impact on student learning. It is essential that we "see learning through the lens of the student". If the learning is not reflected in the student's work, we need to adjust our teaching. Student work is truly at the centre of the instructional core.

- Critical thinking skills, developed through student engagement in the learning process, are one of the greatest purposes of education.

Some of you are using Daily Five and Writer's Workshop. This method of teaching writing is supported in our Language documents and outlined thoroughly in the EQAO Summary of Results and Strategies for Teachers. The expectation is that we will continue this work and set goals for this year in our Professional Learning meetings.

The three-part math lesson helps us to be intentional about our teaching of math. And although there will be skills and process lessons, the majority of our teaching of math will be focused on deconstructing the expectations and engaging our students in the problem-solving model of teaching math, which values teacher judgment and student voice.

We will have two Student-Led Conferences to go with report cards. The conferences will consist of student collections of work and portfolios. Student-led conferences are meaningful and effective assessment/learning opportunities.

Teacher collaboration and student work are key to successful strategies and practices. We will always look for ways to support each other and I welcome suggestions that would allow co-planning and co-teaching, with a strong focus on student work.

Perhaps most importantly, we need to be evidence- informed about student growth and seek to answer the challenge put forth by Hattie – Know Thy Impact.

→ AND WE ARE OFF!

REPORT CARDS AND EVALUATION

The report card should indicate the child's strengths and weaknesses. Comments should reflect this in an individual way, especially in the areas of Math, Language Arts and Learning Skills; not all students are the same. Next steps should indicate means of supporting strengths or addressing weaknesses. They should not be statements of the curriculum areas that will be taught next. The In-school Education Committee, Special Education Resource teacher, principal, etc. can be of assistance. Every child should be successful. Some children will take longer than others.

Please note that comments about students, teachers and parents can be damaging. Please ensure that discussions are kept at a minimum and are held in private. Be cognizant of the Privacy Act.

Please do not discuss children, their parents, other children and other parents within your classroom. Professionalism is a must!

Every child's day must begin with a clean slate. Discuss concerns with me and together we will determine our next step. We all must adhere to the proper procedures.

COMMUNICATION

It is important that I am made aware of any situations that arise. If there is a need for my signature on correspondence, please see me to discuss the problem. Copies of your informational letters should be sent to the office. Keep parents informed of good news and bad news. Contacting parents regularly through positive phone calls, agendas or notes opens the lines of communication.

This year, we will make positive phone calls to each of our students each month.

ADMINISTRATION OF PRESCRIBED MEDICATION

Following the policy on the administration of medication, requests will be forwarded to the principal for approval. Parents must complete and sign the necessary documentation and have one form completed by their doctor. All medication will be stored in a locked cabinet in the office.

→ AND WE ARE OFF!

ALLERGY ALERTS

Please read all student information forms that are returned during the first few weeks of September and note any allergy or medical concerns. Severe allergy alerts are to be posted on the wall in the staff room and by the individual's classroom door, using the templates enclosed. Please also inform the secretary and principal of any severe (anaphylactic) allergy or medical concerns.

Nut and peanut products are not to be brought to school, due to several severe student allergies.

DISCIPLINE: PLEASE BE CONSISTENT!

For the most part, students respond to us in a respectful manner. When you do have a problem, discuss the matter with the student privately and as soon as possible. A quick time out may be necessary. No student should be left in the hall unattended. Have a "buddy" teacher you can exchange students with when a student needs "an alternative workspace" for a period of time. This can defuse many situations without being seen as punitive.

Ensure that the student understands the problem and remind the student of the classroom or playground rules.
If you require the principal's assistance, please call the office to ask me to come to the room. Do not leave your classroom unattended.

Together, we will find a solution to the problem. Each classroom teacher should keep a simple logbook, not only for record keeping and for discussion with parents, but also for special education identification. We need approximately six months of documentation to help us in identifying students', if a situation continues. An incident form should be filled out and submitted to the office for serious or repeat incidents.

MOVEMENT IN HALLS

Students should walk on the right side of the hall, no more than two abreast. The noise level should be kept to a minimum. Students must be supervised. Extra time spent establishing and enforcing these procedures at the beginning of the year will be well worthwhile!

→ AND WE ARE OFF!

VISITORS IN THE SCHOOL

All visitors must sign the Visitor's list and check in at the office upon their arrival. If you notice someone whom you do not recognize, check in with the person to see if they have reported to the office. All doors will be locked while students are in class.

FORMS

Standardized forms are required for the following:

1. Accident Report – Injuries to students that require or may require medical attention. Parents are to be contacted, using emergency phone numbers if necessary. They will advise us of any further action. The form should be completed by the supervising teacher and given to the secretary to type.
2. IT Repair – Any IT/computer equipment that may require repairs are to be completed electronically.
3. Driver Vehicle Registration – Any adult, teacher, parent, etc., driving students on behalf of the school to sporting events, tours, etc. needs to
4. provide us with the necessary insurance information. Check with the office to see if the form has been completed.
5. Curriculum Day Tours – Required for all classroom outings outside of the school. This form is completed by the teacher two weeks prior to the event and given to the principal for approval.
6. Health and Safety Hazard – To be completed when there is a health or safety concern. Discuss the issue with the principal/vice principal and/or caretaker to see if we can solve the problem internally.
7. Leave of Absence – As outlined in the staff's contract.
8. Administration of Prescribed Medication – To be completed by the parent and doctor.
9. Children's Aid Society – To be completed by the teacher when you think there is a case of child abuse.
10. Worker's Compensation – All injuries to staff must be reported to the principal immediately.
11. Safe Schools Incident Reporting Form
12. Workplace Violence Incident Report

HEALTH AND SAFETY

Health and Safety is everyone's responsibility so thank you for reporting any concerns or questions to me or our Health and Safety Committee.

→ AND WE ARE OFF!

SPECIAL EDUCATION AND LEARNING RESOURCE SUPPORT

We are lucky to have such a dynamic In-school Committee system. Each division will meet once per month with the Principal and SERT to discuss any student concerns. These dates are on our school calendar for your planning. Please refer to the following resources to help plan for all students in your classroom:

HOW TO BE A BUCKET FILLER

I will be around the first week of school to read this in every room. Each classroom has their own copy and we have signage up in the hallways as gentle reminders.

CHOOSING CIVILITY BY P.M.FORTIN

I was hoping all of you would have been able to give this a quick read over the summer. Particularly recovering from the global pandemic, the more we can demonstarte how we treat each other with gentleness, respect and kindness the quicker the recovery process.

THE HEART OF EDUCATION BY DARA FELDMAN

A reminder why we chose this profession and what a critical role we play in the future of our communities.

LEARNING FOR ALL

K-12 describes educational approaches that are based on one of the most important findings of educational research since 2000 - namely, that all students learn best when instruction, resources, and the learning environment are well-suited to their particular strengths, interests, needs, and stage of readiness. Like the School Effectiveness Framework (SEF), this guide focuses on ways in which teachers and/or teams of educators can plan and provide the kind of assessment and instruction that enables all students to learn best. Three elements - personalization, precision, and professional learning - are critical to the process.

ONTARIO'S INDIGENOUS EDUCATION STRATEGY

Several resources have been released to help you integrate aboriginal perspectives into your program. Specifically, Implementation Plan 2014, Ontario First Nation, Metis and Inuit Education Policy Framework. This curriculum contains Aboriginal perspectives as well as teaching strategies related to these expectations that you can use immediately in the classroom. The resource is online as well (which may be a better source because it is updated as it has evolved A LOT).

⟶ AND WE ARE OFF!

GENERAL HOUSEKEEPING

1. No students are permitted in the supply room unless supervised by an adult.
2. Keep the supply room, staff room and sports cupboard as neat as possible.
3. Notices are to go home in the Tuesday folders.
4. Students are not to be in classrooms, library or the gym, etc. at any time unless supervised by a teacher.
5. Halls are to be cleaned of shoes, bags, coats, etc. Have students place these articles on hooks or on shelves before heading home each day.

"A hundred years from now it will not matter what my bank account was, the sort of house I lived in or the kind of car I drove, but the world may be different because I was important in the life of a child."-- Forest Witcraft

THANK YOU FOR BEING SUCH A GREAT ROLE MODEL AND FOR TEACHING ALL OF STUDENTS CARING, COMPASSION AND RESPECT THROUGH ROLE MODELLING!!

(They are going to be taking care of me at the Old Age Home –I hope they are kind!)

Family Handbook

Family

HANDBOOK

✓ PURPOSE OF INFORMATION BOOKLET

The main purpose of spending time at school is to gain the academic knowledge and skills that will help you to succeed in the future. In order to accomplish this goal, we must work co-operatively as members of a team. We need to have rules and ways of doing things that everyone understands so that we know what is expected of each of us as we go about our daily work.

✓ PRINCIPAL

add a brief bio about your Principal

✓ VICE PRINCIPAL

add a brief bio about your Vice-Principal

✓ CONTACT INFORMATION

Address:
Phone #:
Email:
Website:

✓ FOLLOW US

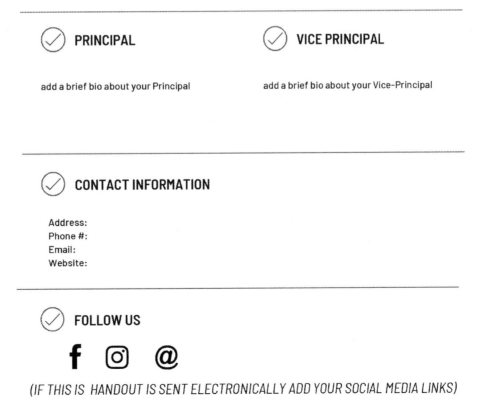

(IF THIS IS HANDOUT IS SENT ELECTRONICALLY ADD YOUR SOCIAL MEDIA LINKS)

→ PRINCIPALS MESSAGE

Dear Parents, Guardians and Community:

Welcome to a great year at (your school name) School! I am thrilled to be the Principal of (your school name). We are still overcoming the changes in our routines due to COVID. We are taking all the precautions we can to make the school environment safe. We will do our best to keep the students socially distanced. Each student will be encouraged to hand wash often, wear their masks and to use the hand sanitizer available in each classroom. This will be a learning curve for all of us, but with your child's cooperation, we will resume school as a welcoming learning environment.

As the administrative team at (your school name), we are so fortunate to work at a school where the community works very closely with the staff to provide the best learning opportunities for each of our students!

As a staff, we welcome you to a great year at (your school name) School! We hope everyone had some fun and rest over the summer.

We currently have a pupil enrolment of 450 students, ranging in age from 3-1/2 to fourteen.

Our school staff works hard to make (your school name) a friendly, caring place where our main concern is providing the very best possible education for each child. We cannot do this alone. The more parent involvement, the better. Our staff **STRONGLY** believes that the more parents are involved, the more motivated our students. Research has proven over and over again that students achieve better results when learning is valued by both the school and parents working together. Parent involvement is THE #1 predictor of student success. We welcome your involvement and support!

This booklet will help you know what is happening at our school. Please feel free to contact the school with any concerns or questions. We have a suggestion box outside the office on the table near the drinking fountain, and we are always looking for ways to make our school the best it can be. Please don't hesitate to drop your suggestions in our box at any time.

Yours truly,

Information Booklet
CONTENTS

Education with a Purpose

OUR
VISION

We are a Bucket Filling School. We try hard every day to fill each other's buckets. (We try very hard not to "dip".)

This is a great spot to include your School's Vision statement!

ZAIRE ELLIOTT
Principal

ALICIA MOORE
Vice Principal

OFFICE ADMINSTRATION

Joy Hayley
Drew Brown

PRIMARY GRADES

J/K - Lisa Brown
S/K - Lisa Brown
Grade 1 - Lisa Brown
Grade 2 - Jane Harley

JUNIOR GRADES

Grade 3 - Lisa Brown
Grade 4 - Jane Harley
Grade 5 - Bob Buffet

INTERMEDIATE GRADES

Grade 6 - Lisa Brown
Grade 7 - Jane Harley
Grade 8 - Bob Buffet

ADDITIONAL TEACHING STAFF

French - Lisa Brown
Release - Jane Harley
Art - Bob Buffet

SUPPORT STAFF

Noon Hour Assistants
Caretakers/Custodians
Library Technician
Instructional Lead
Resource

SUPPORT STAFF

School Counsellor
Care and Treatment
Parent/Family Center

EA/ECE/CYW/ELKP

Joy Hayley
Drew Brown

OUR STAFF ↑

Supervising Teachers are on the playground 15 minutes before entry at 8:35 a.m. and during recess breaks. For the safety and welfare of your children, your children should not arrive at school until just prior to entry times. If your child arrives at school earlier than 8:35 a.m. or leaves later than 3:35 p.m., please make arrangements. Students will be allowed early entry when weather conditions make staying outside from 8:35 to 8:50 a.m. uncomfortable. Special activities may require early return or early entry. This is done only with the permission of the supervising staff member.

BELL SCHEDULE

First Block of Classes
8:50 to10:30 a.m.

Nutrition Break 1
10:30 to 10:50 a.m.
Recess 10:50 to11:15

Second Block of Classes
11:15 to 12:55 p.m.

Nutrition Break 2
12:55 to 1:15 p.m.

Recess
1:15 to 1:40 p.m.

Third Block of Classes
1:40 to 3:20 p.m.

Final Dismissal
3:20 p.m.

Life at
OUR SCHOOL ↑

SCHOOL EXPECTATIONS

Courteous Behaviour is ALWAYS Expected

Classroom
- Show respect for everyone!
- Listen to each speaker.
- Keep hands and feet to yourself.
- Walk.
- Listen to directions and follow them.
- Report anything dangerous or destructive immediately.
- Attend school regularly.
- Come to class prepared to be involved.
- Make up assignments after absences. (Partner with a "Study Buddy")
- Complete assignments and turn them in on time.
- Rely on staff to deal with problems if you cannot resolve them yourself.

Playground
- "Hands off" means HANDS OFF.
- All equipment is to be used in the way it was designed.
- Use appropriate language.
- Share
- No fighting, or "play fighting".
- Stay within the boundaries.
- Things on the ground (sticks, stones, snow) stay on the ground.
- No spitting.
- Use common sense.

Lunch Students
- Use polite manners.
- Use indoor voices.
- Remain seated until excused.
- Clean up your area when finished.

Hallways
- Speed Limit: WALK!
- Stay on the right-hand side of the hall.
- Do NOT disrupt classes in session.
- Respect the displays of student work.
- Walk around people, not between them.
- Use indoor voices.

Bathrooms
- Use, Flush, Wash!
- Return to your class as soon as possible.
- Use indoor voices.

School
EXPECTATIONS

SCHOOL EXPECTATIONS CONT.,

Lunch Expectations

Parents who drop off lunches are encouraged to have them at the school prior to 10:30 a.m. to avoid unnecessary phone calls home. Please do not send glass containers in your child's lunch. We are also a nut-free school. Parents and children are reminded that eating lunch at school is a privilege and we expect all students to follow lunch time rules: be polite inside and wait until dismissal to put rubbish in the garbage bin.

Bus Transportation – Bus Behaviour Expectations

- The Bus Driver must not be distracted by behaviour. He/she must be able to give their FULL ATTENTION to driving.
- Students shall maintain appropriate behaviour on the bus and abide by the following guidelines. These and other infractions by students may result in a loss of riding privileges.
- Use assigned bus stop and proper crossing procedure.
- Be on time (10 minutes before pick-up time) and board in an orderly manner.
- Remain seated, face forward, and share seat.
- Use proper volume (no shouting, screaming or whistling).
- Demonstrate proper behaviour (no fighting, pushing, hitting or kicking).
- Use appropriate language.
- Keep all body parts and belongings to self and inside the bus.
- Keep aisle clear. All carry-on items will be held on lap.
- Refrain from eating, drinking and/or chewing gum on the bus.
- Follow instructions of adult on bus.
- Keep the bus clean (no littering).
- No students are allowed to get off the bus after they have loaded.

Major misconduct will result in suspension from transportation.
- 1st Bus report - one day off the bus
- 2nd Bus report - 3 days off the bus
- 3rd Bus report - 5 days off the bus
- 4th Meeting with parents, child, Principal and Bus Driver

IF YOU HAVE ANY CONCERNS, PLEASE DO NOT HESITATE TO CONTACT
THE BUS LINES DIRECTLY.

School
EXPECTATIONS

SCHOOL EXPECTATIONS CONT.,

ATTENDANCE & PUNCTUALITY

Regular school attendance is essential for learning. Students may be excused from school in case of illness, family emergencies, or for religious reasons. If students are late for class, they disrupt the learning situation for other students and teachers. Students are expected to check in at the office if they are not on time. Punctuality is important and shows consideration for other people.

Our **Safe Arrivals Program** requires the parent or guardian to contact the school if a child will be delayed or absent, if the child is required to leave early or is being picked up by another individual after school.

Please call the office as soon as possible if your child will be missing school for any reason. If the school has not received a call, we will make efforts to contact those parents at home or at their place of employment to ensure the safety of the student. Upon the child's return to school, a notice should be sent stating the reason for the absence (examples: illness, appointment, personal).

If your child is not going to be attending school or is going to be late for any reason, please call the school at (insert your school phone number here).

This one call can save us many calls a day. The safety and security of your children is a prime concern and this process helps us ensure that they have arrived safely. Our phone has an answering service and is always available for messages. Please leave a message. Our school secretary calls if we do not hear from you. Emergency contacts may be called if we are unable to reach parents.

CHANGE OF ADDRESS OR PHONE NUMBER

Please inform the school's office as soon as possible if there are any changes in address or cell or home phone numbers. If we need to contact you in case of an emergency, current information is essential! We know that this is vitally important to your child's health and safety.

PLEASE FILL OUT THE NEW REGISTRATION FORM THAT WAS SENT HOME. We have many changes in cell phone numbers and addresses and contact numbers, we need to insure we have the most up to date information. YOUR HELP IS SO VERY MUCH APPRECIATED. We know it takes 5 minutes to fill out, but we really need it.

Thank you again for your time and support.

School
EXPECTATIONS

GRANDFATHER TEACHINGS / CHARACTER ATTRIBUTES

It is important to foster an atmosphere that supports and encourages self -confidence and
character development. This helps our students to take responsibility for all their words and actions and to be responsible community members and citizens.

September – Resiliency/Perseverance
October – Humility
November – Respect
December – Love
January – Honesty/Integrity
February – Truth
March – Bravery
April – Responsibility
May – Cooperation/Collaboration
June – Wisdom

Every school community member has a right to be in a safe school environment, conducive to learning, and in which he or she feels respected and protected.

Violence occurs whenever anyone inflicts or threatens to inflict physical or emotional injury or discomfort upon another person's feelings or possession. Injury is based on how it is received, regardless of the intent.

No one is entitled to be violent in any form. No form of violence will be tolerated in school, at school activities, on our school buses, or by anyone at this school. Join us in establishing a climate where violence is NOT okay and will not be tolerated.

One aim of education is to promote the development of self-discipline and responsible behaviour.

The staff of (your school name) School foster this development by clearly defining expectations and rules. Most rules are established for the safety and protection of students, staff and school property.

Grandfather
TEACHINGS

PARTNERSHIP: HOME/SCHOOL RESPONSIBILITIES

- Encourage co-operative learning
- promote problem solving strategies
- monitor media content (music, videos, appropriately rated movies)
- promote appropriate manners at home and at school
- promote appropriate language and behaviour
- promote the respect of public and personal property
- encourage home and school communication
- strive for personal excellence
- promote learning skills (see listing on page one of the report card),
- provide support to students (academic, physical, emotional, and social)
- promote academic personal honesty.

CODE OF CONDUCT

STUDENTS' RIGHTS AND RESPONSIBILITIES

- Students and parents shall be informed of the school's expectations for student behaviour and conduct through the School's Code of Conduct.
- Students and teachers shall model the character traits.
- Students have the right to a learning environment that is free from physical, emotional, and social abuse.
- Students shall exercise their responsibilities to:
- Use their abilities and talents to gain maximum learning benefits from their school experiences.
- Contribute to a climate of mutual trust and respect conducive to effective learning, social and personal development.
- Students shall meet the expectations for student behaviour on school premises, out-of-school activities that are a part of the school program and while traveling on transportation that is owned by, authorized by, or under contract, to the Board.

Students shall show respect for:
- Adults and authority figures;
- textbooks & equipment;
- school and Board property;
- others and their property;
- ethnic, racial, religious and gender differences;
- fire alarms and safety equipment; and,
- School, Board and Ministry of Education policies, e.g. Safe Schools.

Partnerships in Education
CODES OF CONDUCT

STUDENTS' RIGHTS AND RESPONSIBILITIES cont.,

STUDENTS SHALL BE EXPECTED TO:

- develop work habits;
- complete homework and school assignments;
- demonstrate good school attendance and punctuality.
- be courteous in tone of voice and body language

PARENTS'/GUARDIANS' RIGHTS AND RESPONSIBILITIES

- Parents shall be informed of the school's expectation for student behaviour within the school's Code of Conduct. This outlines the expectations for student behaviour within the school, on the school grounds, during school activities and on board-approved transportation.
- Parents shall have the right to offer an explanation (in the event of student misbehaviour).
- Parents shall have the right to appeal a suspension of more than one day for a child who is a minor. Parents may not appeal a suspension where a suspension review has not yet occurred.
- Parents shall have the right to appeal an expulsion.
- Parents play a vital role in developing student behaviour and conduct. It is the Board's expectation that parents:
  - be aware of Board policy and the school's expectation for student behaviour;
  - review the Board's policy and the school's expectations for student behaviour and conduct with their child(ren)
  - work with the school to resolve student behavioural issues; and,
  - co-operate with re-admission of the student following a suspension with the school's or Board's recommended course of action prior to the suspension.
- Parents have a responsibility to support the efforts of the school and the Board in maintaining a safe and respectful environment through:
  - reporting to the office first when visiting the school
  - communicating regularly with the school; agendas are available every day.
  - demonstrating an active interest in their child's progress at school
  - supporting Board and school policies and procedures that foster a safe, respectful environment; and,
  - encouraging and assisting their child in following the rules of behaviour.

Partnerships in Education
CODES OF CONDUCT

CONSEQUENCES OF MISBEHAVIOUR

Students must be aware that failure to meet the expectations for behaviour and conduct shall result in consequences that may include some, or all of the following:

- problem solving and review of behavioural expectations
- temporary exclusion of student from class
- behavioural contract with the student
- temporary removal of privileges
- work assignment(s), e.g. school community service
- parental involvement
- detention of student
- referral to a counsellor
- in-school detention
- in-school suspension
- out-of-school suspension – mandatory or discretionary suspension from 1 to 20 days.
- limited and full expulsion from 21 days to a year
- restitution for property damage to an individual or to the Board
- involvement of the City Police

SUSPENSION POLICY

It is mandatory that a student be suspended from his or her school and from engaging in all school-related activities if the student commits any of the following infractions while he or she is at school or is engaged in school-related activities, subject to the mitigating factors below:

- Uttering a threat to inflict serious bodily harm on another person.
- Possessing alcohol or illegal drugs.
- Being under the influence of alcohol or illegal drugs.
- Swearing at a teacher or at another person in a position of authority.
- Committing an act of vandalism that causes extensive damage to school property at the student's school or to property located on the premises of the student's school.
- Engaging in another activity that, under a Policy of the Board, is one for which a suspension is mandatory.

DISCRETIONARY SUSPENSION

A principal may suspend a student because of:

- Persistent opposition to authority
- Habitual neglect of duty
- The willful destruction of school property
- The use of profane or improper language
- Conduct injurious to the moral tone of the school
- Conduct injurious to the physical or mental well-being of others

Consequences of
BEHAVIOUR

ADDITIONAL INFORMATION

SCHOOL CLOSURE

In the event of a power failure or "snow day", please listen to the radio and check face book. We also have a school telephone network to notify you of closures during the school day.

VISITORS

Visitors are always welcome in our school. To ensure student safety and effective building operations, the following guidelines must be followed:

- All visitors report to the office, where personnel will assist you.
- If you wish to meet with a staff member or observe a classroom "in action", please schedule an appointment to avoid disruption of testing or special programs.
- If you are picking your child up for any reason, or if you are bringing him/her to school late, please sign your child in or out through the office.

EARLY DISMISSAL NOTE

If students are to be excused early during the day, please send a note to the teacher.

CONTACTING TEACHERS

We ask that you call between 8:30 and 8:45 a.m. or 3:30 and 4:00 p.m. if you wish to talk directly to a teacher because teachers are involved with students for most of the school day. At other times, a message can be taken and the teacher will return your call.

CLOTHING

Ministry, School and Board policy require students meet acceptable standards of dress and grooming. Being neat, clean and appropriately dressed creates a positive atmosphere for learning. Hats are to be taken off while in the building. Suitable indoor footwear should be worn at all times. Please mark clothing with the student's name. Articles of clothing are easily mixed up unless clearly marked. A lost and found box is available for you to look for missing items.

Your child's safety is important. Hanging jewellery must not be worn in gym class.

SCHOOL DRESS CODE

The following dress code is meant for students, staff and visitors to our school. These are meant to ensure that the respect and safety of the entire school community is established and maintained. Every person is expected to dress respectfully and appropriately for a school learning environment. These are the expectations:

- All hats, bandannas, hoods and other headwear are to be removed upon entering the building (other than religious head dress).
- Midriffs shall not be exposed and halter, off-the-shoulder and spaghetti strap tops are not to be worn.

Additional
INFORMATION

ADDITIONAL INFORMATION CONT.,

- Necklines must be high enough to appropriately cover the chest and tops must not extend below the armpits.
- Shorts, dresses, and skirts should be no shorter than mid-thigh.
- Spike jewellery and chains shall not be worn.
- Clothing may not advertise the use of tobacco or alcohol products or promote drug use.
- Clothing may not include or imply vulgar or suggestive sayings, graphics and/or obscenities.
- Shoes shall be worn at all times.
- Clean and non-marking shoes shall be worn in Physical Education class.

EMERGENCY RESPONSE AND FIRE DRILLS

Regular fire drills and emergency response drills will be held throughout the school year to practice student safety procedures. There are three fire drills conducted in the fall and spring and one Lock Down drill.

EMERGENCY PLAN

We have prepared this information to ensure that you are aware of our procedures in the event that the school must be evacuated or closed during regular school hours. Please familiarize yourself with our **School Emergency Plan** (below). If you have any questions, please do not hesitate to contact the school.

In the event of an emergency in the school, the principal will assess the need for immediate school closure. In the event that the emergency causes the immediate evacuation of the school, students will be moved to the following emergency shelter location: Insert this information here.

Your children will remain at the school **(in case of school closure)** or at the emergency shelter **(in case of school evacuation)** until:

- You make necessary arrangements to have your children picked up;
- Your children can walk home upon parental consent or take regularly provided transportation; or,
- Your children are allowed to walk to the home of the designated guardian.

In the event of an emergency, telephone communication is often disrupted or at the very least, difficult. Therefore, we strongly suggest you attempt to arrange for a designated guardian if you are not at your home during school hours.

Except in the case of inclement weather, regular school bus transportation will be provided to those students who require it.

Additional
INFORMATION

ADDITIONAL INFORMATION CONT.,

NUTRITION BREAKS

Supervision is provided for students eating at school. Our school is fortunate to have four assistants supervising at lunch break. Students eat in their classrooms during these breaks. Students are expected to be responsible for their behaviour and to demonstrate respect for their peers and lunch monitors. Adults are always in charge.

MILK PROGRAM

White and chocolate milk are available for first Nutrition Break. Sheets of tickets for those wishing to take part in the milk program will be available at the office in September. Please order at the beginning of each month.

TUESDAY FOLDERS

Please check you child's backpack every Tuesday. Each student is given a "TUESDAY FOLDER" to help communicate between the school and home. All memos and updates will be sent home on Tuesday in the folder. If there are any changes to our calendars, we will send home a Tuesday Memo to parents with the updates. The youngest in the family will be given notices from the office so that each family only needs one copy of (e.g.This handbook, newsletters, changes in calendar)

MONTHLY NEWSLETTER

Please read your monthly Newsletter to keep up to date on our plans and activities. Sometimes we change dates as the year progresses. The newsletters help us communicate with you. The School Newsletter is usually sent out the Tuesday prior to the first day of each month.

SCHOOL AGENDAS

Each student is asked to bring in $5.00 to help subsidize the cost of our School Agendas. This has proven to be an excellent way for staff to communicate with home. PLEASE be sure to sign your child's agenda each and every night. (Grade 1 right through to Grade 8).
THANK YOU!!! (The more we communicate, the better we can support your child).

MONTHLY ASSEMBLIES

Assemblies are held at the end of each month to celebrate School activities and recognize individual and group achievements. We focus on our Healthy Habits of Happy Kids, Character Attributes and Manners Matter. Please check your calendars for times and feel free to join us!

LOST AND FOUND

We have a Lost and Found box that contains all the items that have been found on the playground, in the classrooms and in the halls. If your child has lost an article, please feel free to come and check the Lost and Found box at any time.

Additional
INFORMATION

ADDITIONAL INFORMATION CONT.,

SPECIAL EDUCATION

The Special Education Resource Teacher at our school is available to provide the following support:

- For students identified as exceptional, a program designed to meet the student's needs is developed in co-operation with the classroom teacher. This program is usually provided within the regular class, but the student may also be withdrawn to work in the Resource Centre as needed.
- Along with the classroom teacher, the Special Education Resource Teacher helps to identify students' strengths and needs and then plans a program of appropriate strategies and resources for any student experiencing difficulties learning.

REFERRALS

Should a concern persist, the classroom teacher may request the help of the In-School Education Support Team. This committee will consider the strengths, needs and interests of the student and suggest program modifications that will help the student to progress and succeed. Both Primary and Junior/Intermediate divisions meet once per month.

The Team may recommend further testing or assessment by other Board staff. As a parent, you will be informed before any actions are taken at this level. It is through this process that a student may be identified as exceptional.

FAMILY ISSUES

Many factors influence a child's ability to concentrate and learn. We want to be sensitive to each student's needs. If your child is experiencing a situation at home that may impact his/her learning, please let the classroom teacher, the student assistance worker or the principal know as soon as possible. Working together, we can provide the support your child may need. Examples of factors: loss of a loved one or pet, new resident in the home, upcoming move, change in family structure.

SCHOOL AND ATTENDANCE COUNSELLORS

Counselling services are available through the School Board to support the work of teachers at the school. If you feel your child would benefit from some help in this area, please feel free to give us a call so the concern can be addressed. Our School Counsellor is available on Wednesdays and Thursdays all day. Sometimes, when a young child is dealing with the passing of a pet, grandparent, a move, or a separation of their parents, the counsellor can be helpful. Please do not hesitate to call the school and ask for a permission form if your child is having issues or a situations they are having trouble dealing with.

Additional
INFORMATION

ADDITIONAL INFORMATION CONT.,

PARENT (COUNCIL) MEETINGS

Parent (Council) meetings help to bring together school, students, families and members of the community to share in the responsibility of our children. Parents provide advice to the School Principal and, where appropriate, to the School Board on a variety of issues, including; curriculum, program goals and priorities, school-based services and community partnerships. Parent Councils are comprised primarily of students' parents and guardians, the school Principal, a teacher and a non-teaching staff member.

The Parent (Council) meetings may include the organizing of fundraising events for the school as well.

Please send the form back to school with your child if you are interested in joining us!! ALL PARENTS ARE WELCOME! We value your ideas and suggestions.

Parent Meetings will meet six times per year. Meeting dates are as follows:
- Monday, September 26, 2022 at 6:00 pm
- Monday, November 7, 2022 at 6:00 pm
- Monday, December 5, 2022 at 6:00 p.m.
- Monday, March 21, 2022 at 6:00 pm
- Monday, April 11, 2022 at 6:00 pm
- Monday, June 6, 2022 at 6:00

SCHOOL RECORDS

A Student Registration Verification Sheet for each child will be sent home at the beginning of the school year. Please complete it if there are any changes to telephone numbers, address, marital status, emergency contact person, doctor, workplace, etc. This information should be reported to the school secretary so that our records are always up to date.

Please only fill in CHANGES in the information we already have, i.e. telephone, emergency contacts

SICK STUDENTS

Our policy is to send students who become ill during the day home as soon as possible. The school will contact parents or emergency contacts and ask that the ill student be picked up or given permission to go home.

Additional
INFORMATION

ADDITIONAL INFORMATION CONT.,

INFORMATION ABOUT THE ADMINISTRATION OF MEDICATION
At times, schools are requested by parents/guardians to oversee the administration of prescribed medication to their child. The School Board requests that, whenever possible, parents make arrangements to administer medication at home. School personnel will administer authorized medication following School Board procedures.

The following conditions apply:
- There must be no cost to the Board/School
- A current Note to School (please ask for these forms at the school office) from you and from
- your child's physician must accompany the request. This must be renewed each school year.
- Elementary students may not carry their own medication, except in special circumstances
- approved by the school, parent, and physician.
- All medication must be brought to the school by a responsible adult and removed at the end of each school year.
- All medication shall be brought in the originally prescribed container with the original labels.
- Inhalers may be carried by responsible students of elementary age. The appropriate Notes
- must be on file at the school.
- Epi-pens and Glucagon, unlike other medications, will not be kept in a locked area of the
- school. Parents are asked to provide Epi-pens for more than one location in the school.
- Students generally will come to a prearranged place for their medication and should take
- responsibility, as appropriate, to go to that spot at the arranged time.
- We encourage parents not to send over-the-counter medication to school. Some of our students are sensitive to the medicinal ingredients contained in such items as cough drops and cough syrup and may inadvertently obtain these from other children.
- Please consider whether your child should remain home from school while recovering from
- severe illnesses.
- Schools, while taking precautions, will not be responsible for loss, theft, or damage to
- medications brought to school

When Should I Keep my Child Home from School?
- Whenever a child complains of not feeling well on a school day, parents are faced with deciding whether or not to send the youngster to school. How do you make the right choice? Generally speaking, if a child is sick, he/she should NOT come to school.
- If your child is vomiting, experiencing diarrhea or running a temperature, please keep your child home for at least 24 hours or until he/she is completely recovered. Should a child become ill during the school day, parents will be contacted to take him/her home.
- If a youngster is sick, but you feel he/she can come to school as long as they stay inside, PLEASE RECONSIDER. A STUDENT WELL ENOUGH TO ATTEND SCHOOL WILL BE CONSIDERED WELL ENOUGH TO PARTICIPATE IN OUTSIDE RECESS.

Additional
INFORMATION

ADDITIONAL INFORMATION CONT.,

LIST OF DISEASES AND INCUBATION PERIODS

Disease & Incubation - Spread - Symptoms - Action Required

COVID
- Air born, discharge through coughing, sneezing, talking
- Sore throat, coughing, heaviness in the chest, headache
- Exclude from school until a negative COVID test can be presented

Common Cold
- Direct contact, secretions of nose & throat
- Runny nose, eyes water, slight fever, feels "bad"
- Exclude from school until recovered.

Chicken Pox
- 2-3 weeks
- Secretions of nose and throat discharges
- Mild fever with small water blisters on skin
- Exclude from school until evidence of treatment (drainage stops)

Influenza
- Discharge from nose & throat
- Fever, distress, aching back, limbs, throat
- Exclude from school. May return when recovered.

Lice – variable
- Infected persons and/or clothing, combs
- Lice, nits on hair shaft and itching
- Exclude from school. May return when lice & nit free.

Scarlet Fever
- 2-5 days
- Discharge from upper respiratory tract
- Sudden onset, usually with fever, sore throat, vomiting, headaches, strawberry tongue.
- Exclude from school. May return after 24 hours of treatment.

Strep Throat
- Discharge from upper respiratory tract.
- Rapid onset of fever, sore throat, tonsillitis, or laryngitis.
- Exclude from school. May return after 24 hours of treatment.

Whooping Cough
- Discharge from nose & throat
- Ordinary cough, becoming persistent, worse at night.
- Exclude from school. May return minimum of 21 days after development of whooping cough.

Rubella (German Measles)
- Rash
- Exclude from school. May return 4 days after onset of rash.

Additional
INFORMATION

SCHOOL ACTIVITIES

September
- Welcome Back B.B.Q. and Class Visits
- Chocolate Bar Sales
- Milk
- Dress Down Contributions to Community
- Alzheimer's Coffee Hour
- Donations
- Little Caesar's Pizza (Sept. 20-Oct. 19)
- Hat Day
- Pizza/Pasta Days
- Sundaes

October
- Book Fair
- Deilman's catalogues
- United Way Donations
- Halloween Family Dance
- Pizza/Pasta Days
- Sundaes

November
- Milk
- Canned Food Drive
- Pizza/Pasta Days
- Crazy Hair Day
- Sundaes

December
- Donations to Food Bank
- Milk
- Pizza Day
- Sundaes

January
- Milk
- Change for Change for Easter Seals
- Pajama Day
- Pizza/Pasta Days
- Sundaes

February
- Milk
- Valentine's Family Dance
- Pizza Day
- Sundaes

March
- Donations at Dance Recital
- Milk
- Pajama Day
- Pizza/Pasta Days
- Sundaes

April
- Milk
- Spring Fling Family Dance
- Pizza Day
- Sundaes

May
- Milk
- Scholastic Book Fair
- Jump Rope for Heart
- Pizza Days
- Hat Day
- Frozen Yogurt
- Sundaes

June
- Milk
- Pizza Day
- My Hero Day
- Sundaes

School
ACTIVITIES

Thank you for all the support you demonstrate for contributing to all our school activities!
We are proud to support our community partners!

SCHOOL FOR KIDS

September Newsletter

VOLUME 1 • SEPTEMBER 2022

THE SCOOP

BRIGHTON ELEMENTARY MONTHLY NEWSLETTER

WELCOME!

MS. DODDS, PRINCIPAL

Brighton Elementary is one of the best schools!! We have a wonderful group of students, teachers, support staff and parents. It's a pleasure to visit all of the classrooms,
We're very fortunate to have such a strong, dedicated team working together for our children.

A HUGE Thank you to our custodial team for making the school so Welcoming, clean and shiny for all of us!!!

This month, we will focus on building the Character Attributes, of
PERSEVERANCE
Aabji-nookiitang gegoo

PERSEVERANCE

Don't give up!
Motivate yourself to keep trying Don't be afraid to fall
If at first you don't succeed try again
Strive for excellence
Set high goals for yourself
Don't give in to hardship

Orange Shirt Day

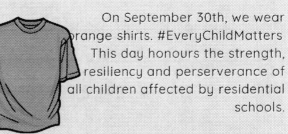

On September 30th, we wear orange shirts. #EveryChildMatters
This day honours the strength, resiliency and perserverance of all children affected by residential schools.

HAPPY Birthday

SEPTEMBER BIRTHDAYS

⭐ JOHNNY   ⭐ JOHNNY   ⭐ JOHNNY   ⭐ JOHNNY

⭐ WILLOW   ⭐ WILLOW   ⭐ WILLOW   ⭐ WILLOW

⭐ RYAN   ⭐ RYAN   ⭐ RYAN   ⭐ RYAN

HOME/SCHOOL COMMUNICATION

Regular communication between home and school is a key element to student success. The school makes every effort to keep families informed of school activities and student progress. Please let your child know that you expect to receive information items promptly when they are sent home from school. A routine of placing their agenda/folder and other information on the kitchen counter or in a special place or basket each day after school can be helpful.

Agendas:
Grade 1 to Grade 8 agendas will go home everyday to help parents be aware of homework and assignments and what is happening in the classroom.
Monday folders:
Monday folders will go home each Monday with school notes, milk, hot lunch forms.
Newsletters:
On the Monday before each month a school newsletter will be sent home to every family with the youngest or only child and is distributed to local businesses and restaurants. It is important to read the newsletters to stay informed about school programs, upcoming events and student accomplishments.

Our grandfathers and grandmothers tell us to honour and respect everyone, especially ourselves, and to realize we also have personal boundaries and the right to be respected

JUST A LITTLE BIT

SCHOOL & CLASSROOM EVENTS

Try setting up and **"in and out"** basket for you child's agenda book, newsletters, notes home and lunch orders. There may be some days when your paths do not cross.

For older student try a shared Google calendar. A few minutes of organizing every day will keep you up to date and help your child be responsible for managing his or her time.

SELF IDENTIFICATION

Establishing baseline data on the achievement of First Nation, Metis, and Inuit students in our schools is key in implementing programs to support our Aboriginal students in the Board. The information from voluntary self-identification will assist the Board with programming enhancements for all our students. Students and parents/guardians who wish to voluntarily self-identify are encouraged to do so by checking the appropriate box on the student registration form that is sent home.

The ADSB Voluntary Self-Identification Policy is located at www.adsb.on.ca.

OUR PARENT COUNCIL

The goal of Parent Council is to help families feel comfortable at the school, informed about school programs, and involved in their child's education. The first Parent Council meeting will be at 6:00pm on, September 25th in the staff room.

Our monthly meetings are informal and generally last an hour. Please come to see if it is something you would like to join us this year! For more information please call us at the school at 705-649-2130.

ALLERGIES

Please remember when you are packing your child's lunch that we have students with life threatening allergies. Their allergies are medical conditions that cause a severe reaction and can cause death within minutes. We ask parents to not send peanuts or nut products to school to eliminate the risk of reactions to these foods. We also have individuals at school who experience serious side effects when they breathe or come into contact with even small amounts of fragrance chemicals. These outbreaks affect their ability to think and work effectively and comfortably at school. We want to maintain our school as a healthy working environment for students and staff. Please help us to be a "Scent Sensitive School" by reminding your child to avoid wearing highly perfumed products to school.

STUDENT FORMS

Please review the forms sent home with each of your children. For your convenience we have printed off the existing information we have, and ask that you highlight any changes and return the form to the school. This ensures that we have the most up to date information for your child. This data is extremely important for our emergency procedures. Please return these to the school by Friday September 6th. Thank you

FAMILY HANDBOOK

Your child will bring home a student handbook on the first day of school. Please review the handbook with your child. It contains important school information, policies, and procedures.

SEPTEMBER 2022

Grandfather Teaching: perseverance

PERSEVERANCE | RESILIENCY

During this month the students are going to be learning about striving to do their best, motivating themselves to keep trying and never giving up on something they want to do. Each class will discuss becoming strong, healthy and successful following difficulties. Orange Shirt Day to celebrate Residential School Survivors will be on September 30th.

Sunday	Monday	Tuesday	Wednesday	Thursday	Friday	Saturday
				1 Professional Development Day	2	3
4	5 Labour Day	6 Welcome Back! First Day for our wonderful students and staff!!!	7	8	9 Welcome Back Assembly (Daily schedules due in the office)	10
11	12 (Supply teacher folders due in the office)	13 Tuesday Folder	14 Staff Meeting 3:40	15 Primary In-School Meeting	16	17
18	19	20 Tuesday Folder	21 Healthy School Committee Meeting 10:40	22 Junior In-School Meeting	23 Professional Development Day	24
25	26 Parent Council 6:00	27 Tuesday Folder	28	29 Intermediate In-School Meeting	30 Orange Shirt Day End of Month Assembly	

Parents and guardians, we are SO HAPPY to have your children with us each and every day! Please let the school know if your daughter/son has any concerns. We look forward to seeing them every day. If they are going to be absent, please call the school and let us know.

Principal's Guide

Use of Calendars and Templates

CALENDARS

The calendars are set out for the school year with all the date details we know before the school year begins. e.g., professional development days, holidays, special teach shirt days (Orange and pink)

In Ontario all our schools are committed to have a staff meeting once per month, and parent council 6 times per year. For parents and teachers, it is much easier to make sure you attend these meetings if you know well in advance of when they are. Teaching parents need to know what evenings they are committed and which days have staff meetings to be able to arrange after school care.

As Principals, I believe that these opportunities to communicate with people face to face are vital to the moral of the school building. There is no reason not to plan these out well in advance and put them on the calendar.

There will be occasions that some meetings or other obligations need to be adjusted. That is why we can make these adjustments every month and send it home on the back of the Monthly Newsletter.

Demonstrating that you value face to face meetings by having them planned and having an organized agenda will translate to your staff that you know how valuable their time is. All your staff, especially the teachers are stretched to the limit. They **NEED** your support. Be available to them on your terms, by having set times for these discussions.

In my experience, once a divisional teacher has attended an in-school meeting, they look forward to them and the team bonding in your school soars. You will see happier faces in the hallways and feel a calmness in your hallways.

PRINCIPAL GUIDE

The following is to assist with the use of the templates

HANDBOOKS

Communicating transparently with staff and families will benefit your entire school building and the relationships within.

Your staff handbook clearly lays out all expectations of your staff. If there are missteps, it makes it easier to go to have the conversation with the staff member who needs a little course correction.

The Family handbook clearly gives all the information about expectations on the bus, in the school and on the playground. Also parents receive a copy of the school calendar so they see clearly when they are invited to the school.

Communication is the key for a happy school community!

PRINCIPAL GUIDE

The following is to assist with the use of the templates

NEWSLETTERS

The next several pages are examples and suggestions of how you can format each newsletter with specific themes, following the Calendars Attributes.

I have provided "how to" guides for each child/family to review on ways they can live out the attributes of the month at home and school as well as a song they can learn and sing as a family and in the classroom to help bring to memory for every student the attributes of each month.

MARG

NEWSLETTERS
SEPTEMBER: PERSEVERANCE

I show Perseverance by;
Encouraging myself to keep on trying

- I do not give up easily
- I set high goals for myself
- I am patient
- I keep up my enthusiasm
- I do not give up

Orange Shirt Day

Wearing an orange shirt on September 30th is to honour and remember the loss of First Nation, Metis, and Inuit children who were stolen from their homes and placed in residential schools.

Phyllis Jack Webstad was gifted an orange shirt from her grandmother when she was 6 years old. It was for her first day of school. All of Phyllis's clothes including the orange shirt on her first day of school. It did not go as her family had expected. As a community on the traditional grounds of the Ojibway people, we will be encouraging all members of the school community who are able to wear an orange shirt on September 30th.

NEWSLETTERS

SEPTEMBER: PERSEVERANCE CONT.,

Perseverance Sing-a-Long (to the tune of Mary Had a Little Lamb)

When you're working, stick with it, stick with it, stick with it.

Keep on going, do you're best. Don't give up!

When you're playing, stick with it, stick with it, stick with it.

Keep on playing, do your best. Don't give up!

When you're running, stick with it, stick with it, stick with it.

Keep on running, do your best. Don't give up!

When you're learning, stick with it, stick with it, stick with it.

Keep on learning do your best. Don't give up!

PRINCIPAL GUIDE

NEWSLETTERS
OCTOBER: HUMILITY

I show humility when
- I set a good example for others
- I know everyone is equal
- I help others help themselves
- I listen well to others
- I make good decisions
- I have the courage to follow my own path
- I take good risks
- I am an inspiration to others

We Take Care of Our Bodies (sung to Itsy-Bitsy Spider)
We take care of our bodies,
We exercise each day.
We aet healthy foods,
And we laugh and run and play!

We take care of our bodies,
We don't stay up too late.
We take care of our bodies,
And each day we feel great!

PRINCIPAL GUIDE
The following is to assist with the use of the templates

NEWSLETTERS
NOVEMBER: RESPECT

I demonstrate Respect when:
- I am polite and courteous to others
- I appreciate the uniqueness of others
- I have self-respect
- I am considerate of others, animals, and the environment
- I take care of the property of others
- I treat others the way I like to be treated
- I listen to differing opinions

Song of Respect (He's Got the Whole World in his Hands)
I have respect for you and me,
It can be easy, you will see.
Have respect for the things you see,
Others, self, and property.

I have respect for you and me,
I show other people the best in me.
I respect my friends and my teachers too.
It's the proper thing to do.

PRINCIPAL GUIDE

The following is to assist with the use of the templates

NEWSLETTERS

NOVEMBER: RESPECT CONT.,

Song of Respect (He's Got the Whole World in his Hands)

I have respect for you and me.

I take care of other's property.

I respect the earth and the animals too.

Respect in everything I do.

I have respect for you and me.

It can be easy, you will see.

Have respect for the things you see,

Others, self, and property.

PRINCIPAL GUIDE

The following is to assist with the use of the templates

NEWSLETTERS
DECEMBER: LOVE

I am Loving when
- I use kind words and actions
- I treat others kindly
- I am concerned about how others feel
- I express gratitude
- I think good thoughts towards others
- I help take care of others who need my help
- I forgive others
- I look at a situation from someone else's point of view

Integrity Song (Three Blind Mice)
Integrity, integrity.
Do what is right.
Do what is right.
Be honest and truthful. Know right from wrong.
Be the best you can be as it says in this song.
You know what is right, be the best you can be.
Integrity, integrity!

PRINCIPAL GUIDE

The following is to assist with the use of the templates

NEWSLETTERS
JANUARY: HONESTY & INTEGRITY

I demonstrate Honesty when.

- I tell the whole truth
- I do not steal
- I do not cheat
- I do not twist or exaggerate the truth
- I do not deceive others with words or actions
- I am honest with myself
- I can be trusted by others
- I mean what I say and say what I mean

Honesty Sing-a-Long (London Bridge)

Honest people tell the truth, tell the truth, tell the truth.
Honest people tell the truth, I am honest!

Honest people never cheat, never cheat, never cheat.
Honest people never cheat, I am honest!

Honest people never steal, never steal, never steal.
Honest people never steal, I am honest!

NEWSLETTERS
FEBRUARY: TRUTH

I demonstrate the teaching of Truth when I
- I speak the truth
- I feel the truth
- I act without regret
- I am sincere with all my actions and words
- I am always true to myself

My Brain is so Very Important (My Bonnie Lies Over the Ocean)

My brain is so very important; it helps me to do everything,
Located here in my head; it's why I can think, choose, and sing.
My brain, my brain; it is so important to me, to me,
My brain, my brain; it is so important to me.

My brain helps me think and remember; my brain tells me fight, flee , or freeze;
It helps all my parts work together, and that's why I just have to say,
My brain, my brain; it is so important to me, to me.
My brain, my brain; it is so important to me.

PRINCIPAL GUIDE

The following is to assist with the use of the templates

NEWSLETTERS
MARCH: BRAVERY

I show Bravery when
- I stand up for my rights and the rights of others
- I face my fears
- I do the right thing, even when it is scary
- I do not give in to peer pressure
- I stand up for my beliefs and values
- I am confident in my ability
- I am able to be different
- I do not let my fear get in the way of my dreams

Wash and Brush (Row,Row,Row Your Boat)
Wash, wash, wash your hands,
Wash them everyday!
That's the way we stay Healthy,
When we work and play.

Brush, brush, brush your teeth,
Brush them twice a day!
That's the way we stay healthy,
When we work and play.

PRINCIPAL GUIDE

The following is to assist with the use of the templates

NEWSLETTERS
APRIL: RESPONSIBILITY

I show Responsibility when
- I am dependable and reliable
- I do what I know I should do
- I do what I say I will do
- I accept consequences for my actions
- I am a good citizen
- I reflect on how my actions affect me and others

PRINCIPAL GUIDE

The following is to assist with the use of the templates

NEWSLETTERS
MAY: COOPERATION & COLLABORATION

I show Cooperation when
- I help others
- I work together toward a common goal
- I solve conflicts peacefully
- I am a good leader and also follow when needed
- I respect others and their unique skills
- I share
- I am able to compromise

Fairness is the Way (Here we go Round the Mulberry Bush)

When we are at school, we share with others, share with others, share with others.
When we are at school we share with others. Fairness is the way!

When we're at home, we do our chores, do our chores, do our chores.
When we're at home, we do our chores. Fairness is the way!
When we're at play, we wait our turn, wait our turn, wait our turn.
When we're at play, we wait or turn. Fairness is the way!

PRINCIPAL GUIDE

The following is to assist with the use of the templates

NEWSLETTERS

JUNE: WISDOM

I show wisdom when I

- Do the right thing
- I am honest and sincere
- I determine my values and what matters to me
- I am consistent
- I am true to myself
- I do not give in to peer pressure
- I do what I say I will do
- I set a good example to others

Monday Memos

Monday Memo Sept 12th- 16th

(Thank you for a GREAT first week back)

This week at a glance:

Monday, Sept. 12
Supply Teacher folders due in the office

Tuesday, Sept. 13
Tuesday Folders go home

Wednesday, Sept. 14
Staff Meeting 3:30-4:25

Thursday, Sept. 15

Friday, Sept. 16

Have a WONDERFUL week!!!!

Signage for Classrooms

Safe

Happy

Hands-Off

Ignore/Give Space

Talk

See a Teacher